SHORT
MEDITATIONS
ON
THE BIBLE
AND PEANUTS.

Also by Robert L. Short

The Gospel According to Peanuts

The Gospel from Outer Space

The Parables of Peanuts

Something to Believe In

A Time to Be Born, A Time to Die

SHORT
MEDITATIONS

"A LIVING DOG
IS BETTER THAN
A DEAD LION"
Ecclesiastes 9:4

ON
THE BIBLE
AND PEANUTS.

ROBERT L. SHORT

Westminster John Knox Press
LOUISVILLE • LONDON

Acknowledgements of copyrighted material are continued on page 143.

Cover design by Teri Kays Vinson

Published by Westminster John Knox Press
Louisville, Kentucky

This book is printed on acid-free paper that meets the American National Standards Institute Z39.48 standard. ♾

PRINTED IN THE UNITED STATES OF AMERICA

04 05 06 07 08 09 10 — 10 9 8

Library of Congress Cataloging-in-Publication Data

Short, Robert L.
     Short Meditations on the Bible and Peanuts/by Robert L. Short.
        p. cm.
     ISBN 0–664–25152–8

     1. Meditations. 2. Schulz, Charles M. Peanuts. I. Schulz, Charles M. Peanuts. Selections. 1990. II. Title. III. Title: Peanuts.
BV4832.2S5226 1990
242—dc20   90-40391

With love for my own
little patch of peanuts—
Sarah, Becky, and Chris!

Contents

Before meals, grace—
Before meditations, gratitude!

Great thanks be to my family, who have gone on living with me, even while I was working on this book! I have been told that when I'm in the writing mode I tend to be distant, dreamy, "out of it," and extremely difficult to get along with and through to. That is to say, even more so than usual. "Be not lost so poorly in your thoughts!" a wife once complained to her husband. My wife sympathizes. But it's love that I've been surrounded with and supported by. And surely in that department, there's no one more blessed than I.

And yet again, there's good friend Ethelyn Bond, who over the years has learned to read my hopeless scrawl even better than I can. I think it's called "automatic reading."

And finally there's Charles "Sparky" Schulz. Who could ask for a better friend than he's been all these years? Not only that, but he continues to let me use *his* work to help illustrate and communicate *my* thoughts. Now *that's* friendship, and I'm very grateful.

R.L.S.

1. What's the Best Thing You Can Do for Yourself and Others?
Know the Bible!

"Jesus answered them, 'How wrong you are! It is because you don't know the Scriptures or God's power.'"

—Matthew 22:29, TEV

When Jesus made this statement to the Sadducees, they weren't discussing little questions. They were discussing some really big ones. These are the only questions the Bible and Jesus are interested in—the really big ones. For the most part, they are interested in meaning, not in means. They discuss ultimates, not penultimates. The author of the book of Revelation talks about "the four corners of the earth" (Rev. 7:1, 20:8). Does this mean that John thought the earth was shaped like this page, flat with four corners? Maybe so. Maybe not. Apparently the question didn't bother him very much, or he would have mentioned it. No, John wasn't interested in the physical shape of the world but in the *spiritual* shape the world was in. We're asking the Bible the wrong questions when we come to it with our *little* questions. Its purpose is to answer the questions that really bother us the most and are the hardest for us to handle.

None of us can escape these big questions any more than we can escape seeing Woodstock's single giant question mark here.

11

These questions are to us what this question mark is to Wood-stock: bigger than we are. They are also over our heads. Never-theless, most of us are forced to come up with at least some provisional answers for these big nonprovisional questions. But what if our answers are wrong? This would mean we'd be basing our entire lives on something that wasn't true. We'd be embark-ing on a long trip, but sailing on the wrong ship. And in the case of others, we'd constantly be supplying them with incorrect in-formation.

When Snoopy attempts to write a book on theology, he hits on what he considers the perfect title: "Has It Ever Occurred to You That You Might Be Wrong?" Good question. This is the first question of all good theology. "How do we know right from wrong?" "How do we know the truth?" Or *"Can* we know the truth?" Also, notice this: Jesus didn't say, "In my humble opin-ion, it seems to me that you may be somewhat mistaken"; or, "Perhaps we should all think about this a little more." No, he said bluntly, "How wrong you are!" You are wrong because your *knowledge* is inadequate; "You don't know the Scriptures or God's power." Evidently, for Jesus, these were the two sources that held the answers to life's really *big* questions. If he's right, and we don't want to be wrong, then obviously this is the best thing we can do for ourselves: *Know the scriptures!*

Shouldn't we also know God's power? Yes. But this is not anything we can do for ourselves. If it were, this would be a power we could control. It would not be *God's* power, but *ours.*

2. What's the Best Way You Can Help Your Church?
Know the Bible!

"These are written that you may believe that Je-sus is the Christ, the Son of God, and that believing you may have life in his name."

—John 20:31

American theologian James D. Smart wrote a lot of wonderful books during his lifetime. One of his last was one of his best. It's called *The Strange Silence of the Bible in the Church.* The title itself speaks volumes, the book being a sort of late warning signal to the churches. "I am convinced," he said, "that the mounting ignorance of the contents of the Bible among members of the church . . . constitutes *the* crisis beneath all the other crises that endanger the church's future."[1] But what could Smart possibly mean by our "mounting ignorance of the contents of the Bible"? Surely no self-respecting member of any church could be put on the same level with Sally Brown here. But then it's hard to say nowadays.

The job description of the churches is really very simple: that as a result of their witness to Christ, all people "may have life, and have it abundantly" (John 10:10); that people "may believe that Jesus is the Christ, the Son of God, and that believing . . . may have life in his name" (John 20:31). But if this is actually the commission that Christ has given to his own followers, the churches, it's easy to agree with Lucy that there's been a terrible breakdown of responsibility somewhere.

Again, the job of the churches is to go into all the world and proclaim the good news—the gospel—that's been entrusted to them. But between the churches and the world there's one essential step that must never be omitted, or else all of us are in deep trouble. Our verse from John indicates what this step must be: "These are written that you may believe that Jesus is the Christ, the Son of God, and that believing you may have life in his name." *These are written!* That is, the only knowledge the churches have of their gospel, Jesus Christ, comes through what the biblical authors have written. Therefore, not knowing the Bible really amounts to not knowing Jesus the Christ. It's about this simple: When memory of the biblical testimony withers away, belief in Christ will also wither away. Or, as Smart has put it:

The revelation of God . . . is not to be equated with a book, but it comes to us only through the medium of that book and, when the book is no longer read and understood by Christians, they have been cut off decisively from the roots of their distinctively Christian existence.[2]

So what's the best thing that you personally can do for your church? Know the Bible! This is because *"Somebody's not doing his job!!!"* And I believe it's clear who this somebody is and what this job should be. We have met the enemy, as Walt Kelly's Pogo said, and the enemy is us. So if someday we again begin to do our job, maybe Lucy's shrillness and unhappiness can be considerably diminished; and at that time perhaps we can look forward to a much more hopeful book being published, called "The Strong Clear Voice of the Bible in the Church." If this happens, not only will Lucy's happiness be much greater, but the churches will be infinitely stronger. That's because they'll be doing their job.

3. What's the Best Way You Can Have a Good Education? Know the Bible!

"Jesus told them another parable. 'The kingdom of heaven is like leaven which a woman took and hid in three measures of meal, till it was all leavened.' "
—Matthew 13:33

"A little yeast leavens the whole lump."
—Galatians 5:9

This has actually happened in what we call Western civilization. The little yeast of the Bible and its message has been implanted in certain areas of the world until this entire lump has risen and become a civilization often known as Christendom. This civilization has been plagued with some very troublesome empty spaces in it, of course, but it is still an identifiable unit— a lump. And through it all, the basic common denominator, the glue that has held it together, the leaven that has made it rise, is the Bible. The Bible has furnished, and still furnishes, the basic, most fundamental building blocks of Western civilization. Therefore, this is true: If you live in this civilization and don't have a fair knowledge of the Bible, you are *basically uneducated.* You may know a lot of things, but you won't have the foggiest notion of where all these things came from, what they all mean, how they are interrelated, what to use them for, and generally what makes them tick. You'll be living in this lump of dough without the slightest idea of whether the lump is dough or a malignant tumor. You may have Ph.D.'s in five separate fields, but if you don't know the Bible you'll be an uneducated Doctor of Philosophy. You'll be a barbarian trying to live in civilization. In our time there's a lot of talk about the need for "cultural literacy." There's even a best-selling book by this title; its sub-title is "What Every American Needs to Know."[3] Well, insofar as we don't know this text, the Bible, that has made us what we are, we are cultural *illiterates* of the most basic sort.

And what are the results? Sometimes they can be amusing, like this:

Hilarious! But far more often the results of biblical illiteracy (simply not *knowing* the Bible, quite apart from *belief*) are not amusing at all. The brilliant literary critic George Steiner has made the following observations about these results:

> As any high-school or college teacher will testify, allusions to even the most celebrated Biblical texts now draw a blank. One is, indeed, tempted to define modernism in Western culture in terms of the recession of the Old and New Testaments from the common currency of recognition. Such recognition, most notably in the Anglo-Saxon world and in that of Lutheran creeds everywhere, was the sinew of literacy, the shared matter of intellect and of sentiment from the late sixteenth century onward. The King James Bible and the Luther Bible provided much of our civilization with its alphabet or referential immediacy, not only in the spheres of personal and public piety but in those of politics, social institutions, and the life of the literary and aesthetic imagination. That alphabet knits the poetry of Milton to the prose of Abraham Lincoln; it makes the messianic tracts of Trotsky kindred to the politics of spirit in Carlyle and in Ruskin, to the grammar of prophecy in Emerson. . . .
>
> In respect of [language] the impoverishment has been drastic. But in essence the bite is political and social. In the English-speaking states and communities, some knowledge of the Bible—grounded in the home, in the Sunday school, in the sermon, in the ambient air of recognition—was a bond between classes, ethnic groups, and those within and without formal religious denominations. This shared legacy underwrote the primary images of justice, of communal destiny, of responsibility in observing the covenant of caring which are instinct to democracy. . . . The lapse of the scriptural from the everyday in the commerce of ideas and proposals, of warning and of promise in our body politic in the West entails a veritable breakdown of solidarity, of concord within dissent. The fragmentation of discourse is precisely that of Babel.[4]

Or, to put the whole thing in a somewhat "shorter" form: If we don't know the Bible, we end up back at Babel, and our next production, "The Owl and the Fussy Cat," will no doubt be more thoroughly mixed up than the one before it. Very funny in a cartoon, perhaps, but otherwise an unmitigated disaster.

4. What's the Best Way You Can Help Your Country, Your Society, Your Culture, and Your World? Know the Bible Well and Help Others Know It!

"How little faith you have! No, do not ask anxiously, 'What are we to eat? What are we to drink? What shall we wear?' All these are things for the heathen to run after, not for you, because your heavenly Father knows that you need them all. Set your mind on God's kingdom and his justice before everything else, and all the rest will come to you as well."
—Matthew 6:30-33, NEB

It's no accident that the Bible has had such amazing leavening power throughout the world. Jesus commanded his followers that "this gospel of the kingdom . . . be preached throughout the whole world, as a testimony to all nations" (Matt. 24:14).

> Go therefore and make disciples of all nations, baptizing them in the name of the Father and of the Son and of the Holy Spirit, teaching them to observe all that I have commanded you; and lo, I am with you always, to the close of the age.
> Matthew 28:19–20

This meant that the Bible likewise would always be with the followers of Jesus, since—after the original eyewitnesses were gone—the Bible would be the only record available from those witnesses closest to the event of Jesus himself. The Old Testament records the testimonies of those who looked forward to the coming of Jesus; the New Testament is the little bundle of first-hand reports of his having been with us.

And so the Bible contains the gospel, and the gospel is "the good news." It's news because it is knowledge and information that the world, apart from Jesus, doesn't know. "No one knows . . . who the Father is except the Son and any one to whom the Son chooses to reveal him," as Jesus, the Son, could say (Luke 10:22). And this news is good because of what it tells us. But it's also good because *it changes things in the world very greatly for the better* whenever this good news is heard and understood and believed. The gospel, in other words, not only tells us about a great goodness that still remains inside the followers of Jesus and in the future will be even greater for *all* people, but in the meantime this good news makes a tremendous difference for the better *now,* in the world today.

How does it do this? How does the gospel make this world better? How does it happen that, as Lucy once said, "Well-informed laymen make up the foundation of a healthy society"?

Well, when you've been the father of three young children you may actually have the feeling sometimes that our entire society is held together ("stuck" might be a better word) with peanut butter sandwiches. But in my more sober moments I realize that something far deeper is at work.

   I almost agree with Marcie word for word, but I would like to
elaborate her thought just a little.
   Christian faith does indeed produce hard work, strenuous effort, our very best attempts. If it doesn't do this, it's not really
Christian faith. This is because Christian faith is basically trying
to do God's commandment before everything else. And that
commandment is simply this: to make known the love of God
that's known through Christ. So if we have faith, this means
working hard at the business of love. This is why Christian faith
makes people both good and champions of the good. Christians
want to be good themselves, because in this way they hope
they'll reflect something of God's goodness and love. But they
also want to see "good" governments, "good" societies, and a
"good" world for all other people—because these governments
and societies and this world, if they really are good, will better
enable people to be the very best they can be.
   Christian faith also makes people free and champions of freedom. Christian faith frees people from the wretched burden of
worshiping false gods, of living slavishly for some other god,
some other "first love," who will finally turn out to be only a
cruel slave master. So Christians are free from the anxiety, the
hell caused by idolatry. But they also know that they found this
emotional freedom only in the context of being free to decide for
themselves what god they would serve. If some other person or
group of persons forces this choice on me, how can this really be
my faith? And anyway, what kind of good news—what kind of
"evangel"—is it that needs to be forced on someone?

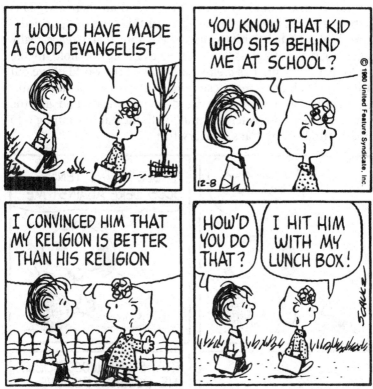

Therefore Christian faith always strives for the greatest possible *religious* and *political* freedom, because it's in this context that the individual's own freedom of choice for Christ is best safeguarded. It's within such freedom that real faith can best be born and grow.

Christian faith also makes people courageous, and champions of faithful courage. If we deeply trust God, what reason do we have to deeply fear anything? This is why "There is no fear in love, but perfect love casts out fear" (1 John 4:18). And so Christian faith is the sworn enemy of the fearful ideas that death is final, that life is meaningless, and that sin and evil will finally triumph.

Faith also contends against all false gods, all superstition, all goblins, demons, and "things that go bump in the night." With the coming of Christ, Christians believe, the divine, the supernatural, is only found *here*—in Christ—and nowhere else. This is the major reason why it wasn't until this type of "purified," more biblical Christianity came to the fore that *science* really began to make progress and obtain a strong foothold in the world. Faith in Christ as *alone* the divine in the world drove out of the world all other manifestations of the divine or supernatural. In this way people were freed to investigate and use the world and the "completely natural" without fear of running into supernatural booby traps at every turn.

Christ also gave people a good reason to investigate and use the world: They would do it for *him*.

Going back to Marcie's answer to the question, "What makes this country great?", I would certainly agree that "faith" comes first—for "this country" or any other. And from faith come courage and hard work. But I'd want to add that goodness and freedom also are produced by faith. If people set their minds on God's kingdom and God's justice before everything else, I believe all these other things will come as well, even—eventually—bigger and better peanut butter sandwiches. It's precisely for this reason that the best way you can help your country, your society, your culture, and your world is to know the Bible well and to help others know it.

5. These Short Meditations Are Short's Meditations

"[Jesus] asked his disciples, 'Who do people say that the Son of Man is?' And they said, 'Some say John the Baptist, but others Elijah, and still others Jeremiah or one of the prophets.' He said to them, 'But who do you say that I am?' Simon Peter answered, 'You are the Messiah, the Son of the living God.'"
—Matthew 16:13–16, NRSV

"Be always ready with your defence whenever you are called to account for the hope that is in you, but make that defence with modesty and respect."
—1 Peter 3:15, NEB

It's not possible for anyone to say they *know* what scripture means any more than it's possible for anyone to say they *know* what's going on in my head. That's something I'm not always sure of myself. If anyone—whether brilliant scholar, exalted church leader, or someone in a mystical tizzy—were to claim they knew what scripture meant, this would not be exactly a modest assertion but would come perilously close to playing God.

This, I think, is why Snoopy is right when he tells Charlie Brown that he doesn't know what Ecclesiastes 9:4 means. Is the author, "the Preacher," speaking literally or metaphorically? It must be metaphorically, because how could the Preacher know, having been neither, whether "a living dog is better than a dead lion?" But if metaphorically, what do these metaphors mean? What can we do when we're confronted with the question of what scripture means and there's no objective way of knowing for sure?

Well, what do you know? Scripture recommends that we think for ourselves. Deeply. Seriously. Even "meditate" if we have to. Jesus isn't satisfied when the disciples only tell him who other people say he is. He wants to know what *they* say. "Who do *you* say that I am?"

"What do you think?" Jesus asks, on plenty of other occasions (for example, Matt. 17:25; 18:12; 21:28; 22:42). "Judge for yourselves," Paul liked to say (1 Cor. 10:15; 11:13). "Let scripture speak to *you*," as Charles Schulz has been known to say.[5]

So scripture tosses the question of its meaning right back in our laps. We don't judge it so much as it judges us. All we can do, then, is listen carefully, ponder, consider, meditate, think. We can use the very best scholarship or highest authorities available to help us think about it, but finally we're asked what *we* believe, how *we* respond, what scripture says to *us*. We are told to "be always ready with your defence . . . to account for the hope that is in *you*." "I don't know," Snoopy says when asked about Ecclesiastes 9:4, "but I agree with it!" And that, it seems to me, is exactly the kind of response scripture is always asking us to make: not so much about objective meaning but about subjective meaning—the meaning *we* find in it.

So these meditations on the Bible are *Short's* meditations. They don't pretend to know or to speak for anyone else. Nor can I claim to know the meaning behind Charles Schulz's cartoons. Perhaps some of them haven't meant anything but were only created with the sole purpose of making us laugh. Charles Schulz and I have been good friends for a long time, but I would never think of trying to pry out of him what he "meant" by a certain cartoon. Because scripture, art, and persons (including Jesus) all call on us to relate to them *personally* . . . and "with modesty and respect."

6. The Bible and Peanuts

"All this Jesus said to the crowds in parables; indeed he said nothing to them without a parable."
—Matthew 13:34

From the very earliest times in the churches, there has been what we can call "image-assisted meditation."[6] Why does meditation need the assistance of images? For the very same reason that Jesus used parables. Whether we're talking about verbal images, as in the case of Jesus' parables, or visual images that the eye can actually see, most minds need concrete imagery to help them concentrate on the matter at hand. Without an image, it can be difficult to image-ine something or even to keep our eyes open for very long. And so when the images of the outside world begin to bore us, our eyes close and we enjoy the wild and crazy images inside our heads. The psalmist can say (77:3):

> I think of God, and I moan;
> I meditate, and my spirit faints.

What does the psalmist mean by "faints"? Linus can probably help us out on this.

This is why I always like to use actual, visible pictures whenever I write or speak to a group of people. Give people something they can actually *see,* and it seems to increase their interest, their understanding, and their attention span. Folks have sometimes thought of this technique as being new. But it's not new at all. Jesus not only used the visual in his parables, he also constantly used it in the *actions* of his own life. And as Charles Schulz reminds us, in using dramatic and graphic scenes that taught, Jesus was only using a technique that had been around for a long time:

"People," said Martin Luther, "are captivated more readily by comparisons and examples than by difficult and subtle disputations. They would rather see a well-drawn picture than a well-written book."[7] And thus the Protestant Reformation also pushed graphic communication to a fare-thee-well. Cartoons were particularly popular in early Protestant literature.[8] Luther himself was an absolute master in his use of imagery—both verbal and visual, sometimes strong, sometimes charming and beautiful. And I'll bet anything Luther would have loved *Peanuts*. The mighty Martin Luther stooping to cartoons and humor? Here's just one way he discussed the idea:

> We see that young children and young people are easily moved by fables and tales and are also led with pleasure and love to art and wisdom, which pleasure and love become the greater, if an Aesop or similar masked or carnival figure is presented, who expresses or pro-

duces such art that they pay more heed thereto, and receive and
retain the same with laughter.

But not the children only, but one can beguile also the great
princes and lords in no better way to wisdom and its use, than that
one have fools speak the truth to them. They can tolerate and listen
to them, when they will not or cannot tolerate the truth from any
wise person; in fact all the world hates the truth if it fits them.

For this reason such wise and great people have fabricated fables,
and have one animal speak with another, as if they would say: Now
then! No one will listen to the truth, nor tolerate it, and yet we
cannot get on without the truth, so we will deck it out, and dress it in
gay, false colors, and delightful fables, and though no one will listen
to it from a human mouth, yet they will hear it from the mouths of
beasts and animals.[9]

The Bible and *Peanuts* are excellent go-togethers. As we've
already seen, Charles Schulz enjoys using the Bible in his work.
As far as I know, he was the first to include actual quotes from
the Bible in a comic strip. And Schulz knows the Bible *very*
well—as well as any lay person I know and better than a lot of
ministers. The study in his home could be a minister's study,
with its shelves of biblical commentaries. So it's not surprising
that we get high-potency doses of the Bible with our *Peanuts,*
both in the lines and between them.

Furthermore, the formula Schulz has chosen for *Peanuts*
lends itself to many easy relationships with the Bible—his con-
centration on the basics of life, his only using children and animals (which Jesus many times uses as figures for the kingdom of
God)—and of course there's the entire dimension of humor. For
as we'll see a little later, there are plenty of strong and significant
family ties between hope and humor, faith and folly, Christianity and comedy. Also, we're dealing with the humble medium of
a comic strip. The trouble with fine art and sacred art is that
they have a tendency to become too "fine" and too "sacred."
But a comic strip modestly takes its place among the popular
arts. And if there was ever a book that likewise strives cease-
lessly to be popular and down-to-earth and graphically engaging,
it's the Bible.

7. What's the Best Way to Know the Bible?
Read It, with All Your Mind and Strength!

"But for your part, stand by the truths you have learned and are assured of. Remember from whom you learned them; remember that from early childhood you have been familiar with the sacred writings which have power to make you wise and lead you to salvation through faith in Christ Jesus. Every inspired scripture has its use for teaching the truth and refuting error, or for reformation of manners and discipline in right living, so that the man who belongs to God may be efficient and equipped for good work of every kind."

—2 Timothy 3:14–17, NEB

The Bible is quite clear that God's first commandment to us is this: "Jesus answered . . . 'The Lord our God . . . is one; and you shall love the Lord your God with all your heart and . . . soul, and with all your mind, and with all your strength' " (Mark 12:29–30). And because, as James Smart said of the Bible, "the revelation of God . . . comes to us only through the medium of that book," this means we should approach the Bible in much the same way that we are commanded to love God—that is, with all our heart, with all our mind, and with all our strength.

Starting with the last first, we begin with *strength*. Strength simply means that work is required. The Bible is an extremely rich book—the richest! But we can't expect to benefit very much from its treasures without putting forth effort. "No pain, no gain," as they say. This point would seem to be obvious, but it's not as self-evident as one might think. The Bible itself constantly warns us about the depth of our own spiritual laziness. It tells us we tend to be so spiritually lazy that we can't even *see* how spiritually lazy we are. And therefore the directive to

"Get busy and read the Bible!" will often work about like this:

"The Bible is its own best interpreter!" This saying is so important for understanding the Bible that theological students used to be required to learn it in Latin. How could anyone possibly forget it if it's in Latin? But the statement is true, and it's the reason we should know as *much* as we can of the Bible as *well* as we can. Otherwise it's possible to get a very distorted, one-sided, view of things. As the above passage from 2 Timothy tells us, scripture is not only useful for "teaching the truth," but also for "refuting error." This is why we need to watch out for—and not *be*—"biblical smatterers." Biblical smatterers will quote chapter and verse of their favorite passages but ignore a lot of other things. In the story of Satan's three temptations of Jesus (Matt. 4:1–11), Satan actually uses scripture to tempt Jesus in the second instance. But in all these cases, Jesus overcomes the tempter with the use of *more*—not less—scripture. So the fact that "the Devil can cite scripture for his purpose" (as

Shakespeare can say) shouldn't lead us to neglect scripture; rather, it means we need to *know* scripture better than our adversary does. Otherwise, we could go hungry for a long time.

Does this strength expended on the Bible result in strength for those who participate in this exercise? Our passage from 2 Timothy assures us it will. Among other things, it produces "reformation of manners and discipline in right living, so that the man who belongs to God may be efficient and equipped for good work of every kind." In *Peanuts,* it's Linus who has certainly worked hardest in getting to know the Bible. And notice the strength this has given him: his quickness to protest against wrongdoing and to do something good when he sees something he can do—even if he isn't always clear about what he's read.

Anyone who thinks that we can stop using our *minds* when we go to scripture simply hasn't been there. Just the reverse is true: Nothing can challenge our mental abilities as much as the Bible. Our greatest understanding is called for in finding faith; once faith is found, it joyfully and obediently seeks greater and greater understanding. Just try one of the longer letters of Paul. It'll immediately become apparent that the person we're dealing with here was an intellectual giant. And this means that the people to whom these letters were addressed (including us) aren't expected to be intellectual pygmies, either. For anyone looking for abundant food for thought and amazing intellectual growth, the Bible is the place to go. You'll fall in love with it. It'll become "holy" to you. Its mere beauty will no longer be enough to satisfy you; but the mental exhilaration and sheer joy in its *meaning* will fascinate you and abide with you forever. The Bible reaches out and grabs us with questions (and answers) we could never come up with on our own. It has "power to make you wise."

8. What's the Best Way to Know the Bible?
Read It, with All Your Heart!

"Spiritual truths . . . are spiritually discerned."
—1 Corinthians 2:13-14

With all our *heart,* with all our *head,* and with all our *hand*—this is the way the Bible directs us to serve and love the particular God who meets us in the Bible, and therefore we use this same pattern in approaching the Bible itself. In this pattern we see that the Bible always places *heart* first and *mind* second.

This is important because we all have a natural inclination to reverse this order and hence, as Charlie Brown can say of himself, we "shovel sidewalks, rake leaves, and garble messages!"

If we approach the Bible primarily with our minds, it's really not going to mean that much to us or to anyone else that we might want to approach with it.

In a recent film, *Dead Poets Society,* young English professor John Keating is trying to teach his prep school boys to drink deeply of the joys of poetry and in this way to learn "to suck the marrow out of life." There's an unforgettable scene that goes like this:

> "Boys," he said as the class bell rang, "open your Pritchard text to page 21 of the introduction. Mr. Perry"—he gestured toward Neil—"kindly read aloud the first paragraph of the preface entitled 'Understanding Poetry.'"
>
> The boys found the pages in their text, sat upright, and followed as Neil read: "Understanding Poetry, by Dr. J. Evans Pritchard,

Ph.D. To fully understand poetry, we must first be fluent with its meter, rhyme, and figures of speech, then ask two questions: (1) How artfully has the objective of the poem been rendered and (2) How important is that objective? Question 1 rates the poem's perfection; question 2 rates its importance. Once these questions have been answered, determining the poem's greatness becomes a relatively simple matter. If the poem's score for perfection is plotted on the horizontal of a graph and its importance is plotted on the vertical, then calculating the total area of the poem yields the measure of its greatness. A sonnet by Byron might score high on the vertical but only average on the horizontal. A Shakespearean sonnet, on the other hand, would score high both horizontally and vertically, yielding a massive total area, thereby revealing the poem to be truly great.' "

Keating rose from his seat as Neil read and went to the blackboard. He drew a graph, demonstrating by lines and shading how the Shakespeare poem would overwhelm the Byron poem.

Neil continued reading. " 'As you proceed through the poetry in this book, practice this rating method. As your ability to evaluate poems in this manner grows, so will your enjoyment and understanding of poetry.' "

Neil stopped, and Keating waited a moment to let the lesson sink in. Then Keating grabbed onto his own throat and screamed horribly. "AHHHHGGGGG!!" he shouted. "Refuse! Garbage! Pus! Rip it out of your books. Go on, rip out the entire page! I want this rubbish in the trash where it belongs!"[10]

"Excrement!" is actually the word that actor Robin Williams uses in the film. And then, just as Keating/Williams directs, this page from Dr. J. Evans Pritchard, Ph.D., is unceremoniously tossed in the trash by each kid in the class. The Bible is to be read and understood just as Keating demands that poetry is to be read and understood—primarily with our hearts, not with our heads or by letting someone *tell* us what it means.

As a matter of fact, great stretches of the Bible are poetry. And it's fitting that they should be. Because when God personally begins to invade a person's life, his beachhead is established in our hearts. Our hearts are the connecting point, the point of contact. This is because our hearts are most basic to us and make us what we are. Whatever our hearts seek, our minds and strength, our heads and hands, have to follow. It is our emotions that determine our reasons, not the other way around. This being the case, what Peppermint Patty and poet Oscar Wilde tell us here is absolutely true.

Or, as it's often said, "Christian faith can never be *taught*; it can only be *caught*." "Spiritual truths . . . are *spiritually* discerned," as our text tells us.

And so when we finally catch on to what God is saying to us in the Bible, it'll always be the heart that will first do this catching on. Again, we should read the Bible with our *big* questions, not our little ones. And that means to read it with the questions of our hearts. Head questions, at least initially, tend to get in the way and garble the message. Of course it's always nice to know the "who," the "where," and the "why" of any passage of scripture. And we can be sure that any time these questions are of essential importance, the Bible will fill us in. But in the meantime the Bible's far more pressing concern is that we *just listen*—right now, carefully, seriously—to what is being said. Because, no doubt about it, *not* listening can easily turn out to be far more dangerous.

9. What's the Best Kind of Heart to Have for Understanding the Bible? A Broken Heart!

"I dwell in a high and holy place,
with him who is broken and humble in spirit,
to revive the spirit of the humble,
to revive the courage of the broken."

Isaiah 57:15, NEB

"How else but through a broken heart may Lord Christ enter in?" asked Oscar Wilde.[11] For this very reason, Wilde could also say, "Nothing that is worth knowing can be taught." Like falling in love, the experience of a broken heart can't be taught; it either happens or it doesn't. And unlike the experience of falling in love, a broken heart is an experience we desperately *don't want* to happen. But happen it must if we are to become open and receptive to God's word to us as it flows through the Bible. Without a broken heart we are too busy and superficially content listening to other words. This is why the Bible always directs its message, as in Christ's beatitudes (Matt. 5:3–11), specifically to "the poor in spirit," to "those who mourn," to "the meek," to "those who hunger and thirst for righteousness," and so on. Notice, in the following saying of Jesus, those to whom his invitation is extended. Notice also where he comes to meet them—that is, on their own deep level of lowliness and "humble-heartedness." Because only when we reach this absolute rock bottom can we truly find—and then begin to build upon—this new and deep and rocklike foundation of Christ himself.

> Come to me, all who are weary and whose load is heavy; I will give you rest. Take my yoke upon you, and learn from me, for I am gentle and humble-hearted; and you will find rest for your souls. For my yoke is easy to wear, my load is light.
>
> Matthew 11:28–30, REB

"Sound theology" will always be biblical theology. The Bible has sounded the very depths of human existence, and it's precisely at these depths that it makes its bid to lift the heavy loads we carry.

The extent to which we *need* the Bible's message will mark the extent and depth to which we'll be capable of understanding and appreciating it. When we say that we should read the Bible with our hearts, we mean with the *depths* of our hearts and not on the basis of their hard, tough outer coverings. But what about those hearts that *aren't* broken, the ones that are perhaps only a bit banged up on the outside. Should the Bible then be placed on the outer surfaces of these hearts? Yes. Because unless the Bible is violently forced on people (making a tragic rebellion against it almost inevitable), or is given to people in an unbalanced or distorted way, it's still capable of being very helpful and meaningful on many different levels. The Bible resting on the surface of our hearts awaits the opening—the "break"—that allows it to fall into the depths of our hearts. If and when this break does occur, the Bible will be there, ready to provide the spiritual fulfillment it was designed to provide. Then, when the hard knocks of life continue to knock deeply on our hearts, there'll be someone there to answer. But while it waits for the broken-open hearts, the Bible can still be very comforting to those hearts that are only aware of relatively minor problems.

Again, we don't control whether or not this break occurs. Only God's power can bring it about. But it's a break absolutely necessary for understanding scripture and for experiencing the Spirit of God as it reaches out and grasps us through scripture. Therefore we must know *both*. And thus the statement of Jesus: "How wrong you are! It is because you don't know the Scriptures or God's power" (Matt. 22:29, TEV). But notice that Jesus places the scriptures first in this saying. Knowing the Bible is something we *can* control. And so we are to "remember that from early childhood you have been familiar with the sacred writings which have power to make you wise and lead you to salvation through faith in Christ Jesus" (2 Tim. 3:15, NEB). In the meantime, another power—God's power—is needed to split open our hearts, revealing their deep need for the power of scripture. Indeed, it's the purifying and purging and hellish fires *within* the broken heart that boil down the Bible's message into what is most essential and necessary for us to understand for our hearts' peace.

10. Wouldn't It Be Nice (and Easier) to Have Some Single, Infallible, External Authority to Tell Us for Sure How to Understand Scripture?

Yes, It Would; That's Why We Have So Many of Them

"The Holy Spirit . . . will teach you all things."
—John 14:26

As far as the New Testament is concerned, the final criterion for all Christian truth is the Holy Spirit. The Spirit is the final judge of the validity of all Christian knowledge and teaching. "When the Spirit of truth comes," said Jesus, "he will guide you into all the truth" (John 16:13).

How does the Spirit do this? Does it speak to us in actual words? No. It speaks to us in the comfort it brings to our deepest hurts and questions. This is why the King James Bible often calls the Holy Spirit "the Comforter" (John 14:16, 26; 15:26; 16:7). It's the Spirit's actual personal and comforting presence in our hearts, which finally "teaches us all things." All things? Yes. Even how to pray. "For we do not know how to pray as we ought." It works about like this:

"Romans . . . eighth chapter." Verse 26, Revised Standard Version, to be exact. I mention this because I'd like to quote a slightly different translation of the same verse. I change translations with some misgiving, because I know Charles Schulz prefers the Revised Standard Version. How do I know this? Oh, just a feeling I have. Also, there are bits and pieces like the following:

But please let me quote the Revised English Bible's version of Paul's words: "In the same way the Spirit comes to the aid of our weakness. We do not even know how we ought to pray, but through our inarticulate groans, the Spirit himself is pleading for us."

So whatever deep knowledge of God we may long for, and whether this longing is expressed in sighs or groans, it is ultimately the silent love of "the Spirit himself" that guides us, intercedes for us, pleads for us—teaches us all things through the help and aid and comfort that answers our "weakness." As Augustine could say, "Our hearts are formed for thee, O Lord, and are restless until they find their rest in thee."[12] When our darkened and empty hearts find their rest in God, it is because God has personally come into them. God has come into our hearts in the person of "the Spirit" and there enlightens our hearts with a light and a rest that continue to grow in our hearts, constantly pushing out the darkness and restlessness. Christian knowledge, then, is basically heart knowledge and not head knowledge. It is subjective rather than objective, internal rather than external. It is primarily emotional or experiential or existential, rather than intellectual. Christian knowledge is basically knowledge about love, and the intellect can't even come close to understanding love. "Spiritual truths . . . are spiritually discerned" (1 Cor. 2:13–14).

But this leads to a problem—or at least we usually think of it as a problem—and that is, if "Truth is subjectivity," as Kierkegaard could put it,[13] how can we ever agree on "the Truth" without some kind of universally recognized *objective* standard for knowing the truth? Look at science, for instance. Science has universally recognized criteria for determining truth, and look at the "truths" it comes up with! We can hardly keep up with them. And yet scientists will be the first to tell us that although their method is ideal for determining *means,* science can't really remain science and come up with *meaning.* Science has plenty of "know how," but it becomes religion as soon as it claims to have the "know why." The purview of science is with the provable penultimates, "truths," not with the unprovable Ultimate, "the Truth." For how could one "prove the Ultimate"—since by definition there can be no higher standard of judgment than "the Ultimate" itself? And yet we would all like to see this happen. This would relieve us from the dreadful responsibility of coming up with our own answers for what "the Truth" is. We would no longer need to have something called "faith." Hey, presto! Our faith would then be "knowledge." Truth would be nailed down; it would be *objectively* secure.

And so in the realm of the Spirit we constantly look for some objective authority, something other than the Spirit itself, that will do this for us—that will prevent us from having to find our own answers. "Work out your own salvation with fear and trembling," says Paul (Phil. 2:12). But who wants to do this!? Who wants to fear and tremble? It's much easier to let someone else work it out for you. And so then we set up all sorts of authorities for precisely this purpose. "If this impressive church says it's true, then it's true!" "If this flawless authority or this high priest of psychiatry tells me it's true, it's true!" "If this book, literally interpreted, says it's true, it's true! The truth, the Spirit, is not anything I want a direct, passionate, personal relationship with. I'll just trust in one of these outside authorities to tell me what's true and what's the right thing to do. Just let it give me some idea of the minimum expected of me. In the meantime I can go on with my life and pay attention to 'the truth' only when necessary or when I feel like it." This way we're off the hook. We won't have to listen at all to Paul when he says, "Let every one be fully convinced in his own mind" (Rom. 14:5).

In the same way we try to get around our need for the supremely personal "Spirit of truth" (John 14:17; 15:26; 16:13), the Holy Spirit. We keep someone—or something—around to tell us what to do. For the Holy Spirit, we substitute a "Holy Church," a "Holy Father," or a literally interpreted "Holy Bible" (when interpreting scripture always "is a matter of the heart, spiritual and not literal"—Rom. 2:29). After all, the Holy Spirit is impossible to control and notoriously flighty. Maybe this is why it's always been symbolized by a bird. As Jesus could say of it:

> Flesh can give birth only to flesh; it is spirit that gives birth to spirit. You ought not to be astonished when I say, "You must all be born again." The wind blows where it wills; you hear the sound of it, but you do not know where it comes from or where it is going. So it is with everyone who is born from the Spirit.
>
> John 3:6–8, REB

No one denies the basic human need for ultimate security or salvation. But real security can only come from "the Spirit of Christ" (Rom. 8:9), the Holy Spirit. And it's no more possible to "lock up" this Spirit in a particular church, a high ecclesiastical authority, or a wooden interpretation of a book than it would be to "lock him in the garage!"

The Spirit of God and Christ flows into our hearts through the words of the Bible, and this Spirit itself illumines the book—"the Spirit himself bearing witness with our spirit" (Rom. 8:16).

11. The Bible's Mighty Theme, or "The Bible's Message in a Nutshell" Also: Where to Jump In

"All this has been the work of God. He has reconciled us to himself through Christ, and has enlisted us in this ministry of reconciliation: God was in Christ reconciling the world to himself, no longer holding people's misdeeds against them, and has entrusted us with the message of reconciliation. We are

therefore Christ's ambassadors. It is as if God were appealing to you through us: we implore you in Christ's name, be reconciled to God! Christ was innocent of sin, and yet for our sake God made him one with human sinfulness, so that in him we might be made one with the righteousness of God."

—2 Corinthians 5:18–21, REB

The Bible is obviously the mightiest of all books. Many people will agree with this evaluation, even some who are not great fans of the Bible. But if Melville is right, and I believe he is, what is "the mighty theme" of the Bible? What one mighty theme has produced this mighty book?

This is, of course, an audacious question. Here we have the Bible, with all of its 773,893 words (Linus's count), and yet we're asking, "What is the whole thing saying in just a *few* words?" Is it possible to say in just a few of the Bible's own words what the entire Bible is saying? Is it even a good idea to try to do this? Doesn't this run the risk of dangerously oversimplifying, even if we should manage to isolate the Bible's mighty theme? Also, if we give away the Bible's central message like this, will people bother to read the rest of it? And if the Bible does contain a single, central mighty theme, isn't this something that folks should find for themselves?

These are serious questions, so let me try to answer them seriously. First, no one is compelled to accept *my* answer to the question of what the Bible's mighty theme might be. Anyone whose question this is will finally be required to come up with his or her own answer for it. Second, even if someone should be inclined to accept my answer to this question, it would only be by not taking this answer seriously that they could then neglect reading the entire Bible for themselves, in the light of this theme—and reading it deeply and carefully. And, third, the very nomination of such a overall unifying theme can often help people get into this mighty book with its 773,893 words and its multitude of what can easily seem to be a disparate and very confusing collection of voices.

Anyway, I'm certainly not the only person with a strong opinion about the identity of the Bible's mighty theme. Just watch any big sports event on TV. It often seems that the stands are full of theologians—people with their own ideas about what this theme might be!

Having thus defended myself, I'd now like to make my humble nomination for what I deem to be this theme: It's the text for this meditation from 2 Corinthians. That's it. For me, everything comes together in these few words. There are plenty of other places in the Bible that do this for me too: for instance, Isaiah 53:6 or Romans 8:38–39. But no other passage of scripture quite bowls me over like this one. I'll never forget the experience of reading verse 19 of this passage many years ago. *This is it: the Gospel, the command* I penned in the margin of my Bible. *Bam! Wow! Zap! Boom!* And the years have only tended to reinforce this feeling of love at first sight.

Many people have apparently had something of the same experience. My great theological mentor is Karl Barth. I don't believe there's ever been a person in all Christendom who has had a greater love and knowledge of the Bible than Barth, a biblical interpreter of "matchless penetration," as George Steiner says of him.[14] Here's one of the comments Barth makes about this passage:

> The doctrine of reconciliation is itself the first or last or central word in the whole Christian confession or the whole of Christian dogma. Dogmatics has no more exalted or profound word—essentially, indeed, it has no other word—than this: that God was in Christ reconciling the world unto Himself.[15]

It's nice to find someone so closely in agreement, especially someone with such a powerful name. But in any case this is *my* nomination for the mighty theme, and I'll be using it as a reference point to guide us.

But locating this theme in the New Testament raises one more question before we proceed: namely, in what order to read the Bible. Where's the best place to start? Genesis, chapter one, verse one, or where?

I've never thought it's a good idea to begin with the Old Testament. From the Christian perspective much of the Old Testament is a kind of prologue to the main event—the event of Christ himself. As the New Testament letter to Hebrews says:

> When in former times God spoke to our forefathers, he spoke in fragmentary and varied fashion through the prophets. But in this the final age he has spoken to us in the Son whom he has made heir to the whole universe, and through whom he created all orders of existence: the Son who is the effulgence of God's splendour and the stamp of God's very being, and sustains the universe by his word of power. . . . Thus we are bound to pay all the more heed to what we have been told, for fear of drifting from our course.
>
> Hebrews 1:1–3; 2:1, NEB

For this reason I always advise people to begin with the New Testament. By itself, the Old Testament can seem so remote, confusing, and lengthy that many would-be Bible readers will drift off course before they ever learn what the excitement is all about. The New Testament can certainly never be understood apart from the Old. But the New Testament itself is often adept at summarizing much of the Old Testament in order that people will pay more heed to what they've more recently been told. And thus the Gospel of John begins in exactly the same way as the book of Genesis: "In the beginning." And the seemingly tedious New Testament "begats" deftly telescope all that has gone before. For these reasons I don't think it's a good idea to "just start with the first chapter of Genesis while we're at it." After all, in starting with the Son we really are starting—once more—with the beginning. For "In the beginning was the Word, and the Word was with God, and the Word was God. . . . And the Word became flesh and dwelt among us" (John 1:1, 14).

That's what Christmas is all about. It celebrates the old, old God in brand-new human flesh.

We have said we should let the Bible speak to our hearts. But this should always be a "heart-to-heart" speaking that it does. The Bible indeed contains God's heart-to-heart or person-to-person talk with each of us. And the Bible's own heart is found principally in the New Testament, because Jesus himself is that heart, as Jesus himself attests: "You search the scriptures, because you think that in them you have eternal life; and it is they that bear witness to me" (John 5:39).

12. Christianity and Comedy: Birds of a Feather

"God . . . has reconciled us to himself through Christ . . . no longer holding people's misdeeds against them, and has entrusted us with the message of reconciliation."

—2 Corinthians 5:18-19, REB

Aristotle thought very deeply about things tragical-comical-historical-pastoral, and he tells us that comedy is "what is out of time and place, without danger."[16] The Christian message also tells of something out of time and place without danger—namely, humankind, people, the world. God has already, through Christ, reconciled us—humankind, people, the world—to himself. God no longer holds our misdeeds against us. We're all off the hook! We're finally without danger! That's the punch line, the message, the good news. In the meantime, though, there's obviously a problem. Things are badly "out of time and place." Not everyone has gotten this message, and many who have heard it evidently don't believe it. The fact that many haven't heard it or don't believe it might seem to be a relatively minor problem, and so it is when compared to the goodness of the final resolution of things (see Rom. 8:18). But meanwhile this nonhearing or nonbelief causes one hell of a lot of trouble in this world. (We use the word "hell" here in its most serious theological sense.) And so then, in spite of the fact that all of us are finally "without danger," right now things are in this gosh-awful "out of time and place" mess. But that's comedy. And it's also Christian faith.

What if the punch line were different? What if—instead of being "without danger"—there actually was danger and its unhappy results? Then this would not be comedy we'd be talking about. *With* danger and its negative consequences, we'd have tragedy. Nor would this be the Christian gospel, or "good news," we'd be discussing. *With* danger the "gospel's" good news would only be a grotesque travesty of really good news. It wouldn't be the unequivocal "good news of a great joy which will come to all the people" (Luke 2:10); it would be the bad

53

news of a huge, terrifying, God-designed catastrophe from which only some—perhaps only a few—people manage to escape. So Charlie Brown and Aristotle are right: Whether life is a comedy or a tragedy depends on its final outcome.

As long as we're not sure of the punch line, as long as the final resolution of our lives is uncertain, there's much to be afraid of or disturbed by in this life. But the Gospel bids us "be not afraid" by virtue of the certain totality and the total certainty of its good news about life's final outcome. The entire saying from Luke goes like this: "Be not afraid; for behold, I bring you good news of a great joy which will come to *all* the people; for to you is born this day in the city of David a Savior, who is Christ the Lord" (Luke 2:10–11).

It is only "perfect love [that] casts out fear" (1 John 4:18). But of course the only perfect love is *God's* love, certainly not ours. This is not surprising. We should expect the infinite God's love to be perfect and infinitely stronger than mere human love. And yet even human beings love *in spite of* the beloved's imperfections. Therefore, is the almighty God's perfect love going to be deflected by the faults, weaknesses, and failings—the finite imperfections—of the very creature that God himself has created? We'd better hope not. For which of us really is any better than Charlie Brown?

The good news tells us: Be not afraid! Fear not! The final outcome for all is already assured. It's already been decided. To us a Savior has been born, and we have been reconciled to God through this Savior. But what if you feel you're practically a worthless human being—as worthless as, say, a wretched, miserable little sparrow? In Jesus' time, sparrows were five for two cents at the market. In this case, as a sparrow, wouldn't you have reason to feel disturbed or abandoned, about like this?

 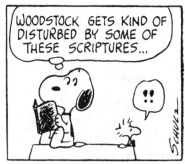

Snoopy has been known to pull Woodstock's leg. Maybe that's why, in this cartoon, Snoopy's not reading all of Jesus' words. Otherwise Woodstock would have heard: "Are not five sparrows sold for two pennies? And not one of them is forgotten before God" (Luke 12:6). And "Look at the birds of the air: they neither sow nor reap nor gather into barns, and yet your heavenly Father feeds them" (Matt. 6:26).

So fear not! For we're assured that God's love extends even to sparrows, a symbol for the lowest of the low. Be not afraid! Because we know through Jesus that our heavenly Father has never created a person he doesn't love—perfectly. "In the world you have tribulation," says Jesus. Things are indeed badly out of time and place. "But be of good cheer, I have overcome the world" (John 16:33). The world is already reconciled to God. Finally we're without danger. That's comedy. And that's also Christian faith. Birds of a feather.

13. The Quality of God's Mercy and Love

"You have heard that they were told 'Love your neighbour and hate your enemy.' But what I tell you is this: Love your enemies and pray for your persecutors; only so can you be children of your heavenly Father, who causes the sun to rise on good and bad

*alike, and sends the rain on the innocent and the
wicked. If you love only those who love you, what
reward can you expect? Even the tax-collectors do as
much as that. If you greet only your brothers, what is
there extraordinary about that? Even the heathen do
as much. There must be no limit to your goodness, as
your heavenly Father's goodness knows no bounds."*
                                        —Matthew 5:43–48, REB

Fortunately for us, God doesn't deal with us on the basis of
law, but on the basis of his love. It's a common misunderstand-
ing of Christianity that it represents some kind of law, either a
new one or an old one. Law says, "It's up to you!" The Christian
message says, "It's up to God and God's grace." Law says,
"People get exactly what they deserve!" The Christian message
says, "Christ got what we deserve!" Law says, "Follow me! I'm
it!" Christian faith says, "Follow Christ! He's it!" Paul describes
the distinction between these two ways of righteousness in this
way: "Of legal righteousness Moses writes, 'The man who does
this shall gain life by it.'" But, Paul says, "Christ ends the law
and brings righteousness for everyone who has faith" (Rom.
10:5; 10:4, NEB).

Nevertheless, history has clearly shown that even in the case
of faith in Christ, there's always a powerful tendency among
Christians to turn faith itself into a new kind of law, or "work,"
and thus to say of faith exactly what the law says: "It's up to
you!" This is not surprising. Naturally self-righteousness is going to be more popular than God's righteousness. But this
means that even in our day, as in the time of Jesus, the woods
are full of "lawyers" who see the relationship with God as being
primarily a matter of law or merit or a righteousness that we can
produce ourselves. Consequently the absolute newness that
comes over people when they really hear the good news doesn't
actually happen. As poet W. H. Auden has put it:

As long as the self can say "I," it is impossible not to rebel;
As long as there is an accidental virtue, there is a necessary vice:
And the garden cannot exist, the miracle cannot occur.[17]

So in the churches, as on the coast of France, when there's nothing really new happening we have a good idea of where a large portion of the blame lies.

Much has been written on Shakespeare's masterful knowledge and use of the Bible. One of the places where Shakespeare does a beautiful job of capturing and expressing much of the essence of the New Testament is Portia's famous "quality of mercy" speech in *The Merchant of Venice*. In this speech she says to Shylock, who stands for "judgment" and "law," that "in the course of justice none of us should see salvation" (IV.I.199–200). That is, if salvation finally came down to a matter of strict justice or obedience to law, of people getting exactly what they deserve, then all of us are doomed. Fortunately, though, God doesn't work this way. Otherwise we'd never see the salvation of God's Son shine on anyone.

The Old Testament's entire book of Jonah is a hilarious spoof of those self-righteous folks (including Jonah) who just get furious whenever God doesn't seem to be dealing with people on the basis of a strict observance of law so that a lot of not-so-righteous people end up getting far better than they deserve. In Jesus' parable of the prodigal son (Luke 15:11–32), the prodigal's older brother is like this. Here's his dad, welcoming home with great fanfare and celebration this ne'er-do-well younger son, while the older brother, who stayed home and did exactly what he was supposed to do, is practically ignored. And then there is Jesus' parable of the laborers in the vineyard (Matt. 20:1–16), where, at the end of the day, each laborer is paid exactly the same wage, whether he worked all day in the blistering heat or only showed up at the last minute in the cool of the evening.

Unfair? Yes, according to human concepts of law and justice. But there's a point behind all this. And that point is: "The Lord is not slow about his promise as some count slowness, but is forbearing toward you, not wishing that any should perish, but that all should reach repentance" (2 Peter 3:9).

God's compassion is a stubborn compassion. Thank heaven for that! Thank heaven that God's forgiveness and love and mercy and righteousness are far stronger than—and will finally win out over—all of the sin and disobedience and stupidity and self-righteousness of us all. And so then, in view of this stubborn compassion of God's, there's still a strong basis for laughter in the world.

God no longer holds our misdeeds against us (2 Cor. 5:19). That's bad news for righteous people but good news for sinners. That is, it's bad news to those who are proud of their righteousness, but it's good news to those who know themselves to be sinners. Anyone who thinks he or she is capable of making himself or herself righteous is going to have little understanding or appreciation for the message of the New Testament. And so Jesus could say: "Those who are well have no need of a physician, but those who are sick; I came not to call the righteous, but sinners" (Mark 2:17; also Matt. 9:12–13; Luke 5:31–32).

"Hide thy face from my sins," begs the psalmist, "and blot out all my iniquities" (Ps. 51:9). And then the psalmist goes on to say, "If you never overlooked our sins, Yahweh, Lord, could anyone survive? But you do forgive us: and for that we revere you" (Ps. 130:3–4, JB).

We live on the basis of *God's* goodness, not our own. And in a sense, God's love is blind. God's "love covers a multitude of sins" (1 Peter 4:8)—our sins. When the father welcomes home the prodigal son, the elder son says, "How can you do that? I don't see how you can kiss such a crabby face." And what Snoopy says about lips is very much like what the father then says about his love for his child.

This love that God has for all of us, revealed once and for all by Jesus, profoundly affects the behavior of those who experience and therefore believe in this love. They are no longer ultimately guided by any kind of written code or set of laws; their single purpose in their smallest or largest deeds is simply to make known this love of God that's made known through Christ. God "has reconciled us to himself through Christ, and has enlisted us in this ministry of reconciliation: . . . [God] has entrusted us with the message of reconciliation" (2 Cor. 5:18–19, REB). The ministry of all Christians is essentially the message. In word or deed Christians are always bent on this single mission: to try to communicate to as many others as possible this love of God known through Christ. And this love, as Jesus says of the sun and the rain, is love for the good and the bad, the innocent and the wicked. God's mercy, says Portia, again echoing Jesus, "droppeth as the gentle rain from heaven upon the place beneath" (IV.I.184). Therefore, this is the way we must try to love also. "There must be no limit to your goodness, as your heavenly Father's goodness knows no bounds."

14. Our Graceful Father and His Children

"What man of you, if his son asks him for bread, will give him a stone? Or if he asks for a fish, will give him a serpent? If you then, who are evil, know how to give good gifts to your children, how much more will your Father who is in heaven give good things to those who ask him!"

—Matthew 7:9-11

It's amazing the influence God's children have over this heavenly Father of theirs. According to Jesus, in the preceding passage, all they have to do is ask and their request is as good as

granted—if not even better than granted. "Our fearlessness towards [God] consists in this, that if we ask anything in accor-
dance with his will he hears us. And if we know that he listens to
whatever we ask him, we know that we already possess whatever
we have asked of him" (1 John 5:14–15, NJB). This is a gloss
John makes on this saying of Jesus. Now what if those who
know themselves to be God's children should pray that eventually God will safely bring home—will "save"—everyone, *all*
people, *all* of his children, the good and the bad alike, just as
God sends rain on the good and the bad alike? But *should* God's
self-aware children pray such a prayer for their fellow children
of God? We have it on good authority that they should. But
wait! John has just told us that for prayers to be heard and
answered by God, they should "accord with his will." Is it God's
will that finally all of these fellow children will be brought
home? We have it on good authority that it is.

> I urge then, first of all, that petitions, prayers, intercessions and
> thanksgiving should be offered for everyone, for kings and others in
> authority, so that we may be able to live peaceful and quiet lives with
> all devotion and propriety. To do this is right, and acceptable to God
> our Saviour: he wants everyone to be saved and reach full knowledge
> of the truth. For there is only one God, and there is only one mediator
> between God and humanity, himself a human being, Christ Jesus, who
> offered himself as a ransom for all. This was the witness given at the
> appointed time, of which I was appointed herald and apostle. . . .
> 1 Timothy 2:1–7, NJB

So here again we hear the news that really is *good* news: *All* will
find salvation and come to know the truth. "There is one God,
the Father, from whom all being comes; towards whom we
move; and there is one Lord, Jesus Christ, through whom all
things came to be, and we through him. But," Paul adds, "not
everyone knows this" (1 Cor. 8:6–7, NEB). And it's just because
not everyone knows this that we have this peculiar ("weird,"
Peppermint Patty would say) bunch of people called Christians
who have been charged with calling people's attention to this
knowledge. God "has enlisted us in this ministry of reconciliation" (2 Cor. 5:18, REB). And because it's God's will that this
eventual reconciliation of all will happen, it *will* eventually happen. What kind of God would God be if he allowed his will for
our salvation to be frustrated by our weak and limited little

wills—wills that the omnipotent God has given to us and directs in the first place? What kind of God? Certainly not a *kind* God. Nor would this even *be* God, having handed his own power over to his creature. The Christian gospel is the "good news of a great joy which will come to all the people" (Luke 2:10). *Will come to all.* In the meantime, what difference does it make that not everyone knows this? Again, it makes a hell of a difference. For starters, people who don't know this great love of God's tend to hate life and therefore easily hate themselves and others. Meanwhile, this love-assured little bunch of people called Christians does its best to open doors, break down barriers, and communicate the message it's been given—the message of its answered prayer: "God bless us every one" and therefore "Joy to the world!"

Paul's writings are by far the most "graceful" in the Bible. By this I mean that the concept of grace is central to the way he develops his thought about the meaning of Christian faith. A quick check in a New Testament concordance will show how frequently he uses the term. For Paul this single word brings together two of God's most essential attributes: God is all-loving and all-powerful. That's grace.

But then a strange thing happens when we switch to the four Gospel writers and check their use of this term. It's found only four times throughout all four Gospels, and all four uses are in three verses of the first chapter of John (1:14, 16, 17).

So what's happened to the concept of grace, so absolutely essential in Paul's thought? If indeed Paul and the four evangelists are talking about the same message, shouldn't we expect the idea of grace to play a major role in their writings also? It does. They just use a different word for it, the word used by Jesus himself. That word is "Father."

In Jesus' use of "Father" to refer to God, the word "father" denotes at least love and power. The father is capable of just as much love as the mother; but of the two parents, the father usually possesses more raw, physical power to back up that love—power to protect the child and to see him or her through to the conclusion desired by both parents. Hence, when we pray to "our Father who art in heaven," we're praying to the God of grace, a grace-full God who is all-loving but also all-powerful.

This is one reason I think it's dangerous to substitute any other word or term for the Bible's use of "Father." This word is theologically loaded with meaning, and to use any other term for it—such as "Father/Mother God" or "Great Ground of Being"—tends to unload it and reduce it to something weak, confusing, and insignificant. Another reason is that it is arrogant and prideful to suppose our modern understanding in these matters gives us the right to ignore or change what the Bible actually says.

But in all of this, what does it mean for us that our Father is a God of grace? It means that finally not one of us will be allowed to escape God's love and salvation. If anyone should finally end up outside of God's salvation, this would mean something had gone wrong with either God's love or God's power or both. It would mean that finally our Father did not love us enough to bring us to salvation, or was not powerful enough, or both. Our Father would turn out to be not so "graceful" after all.

But the Father of Jesus is the God of grace, and this Father—just like those of us who are also fathers—will have his day. The reconciliation of all God's children will come precisely because God wills it. Wishful thinking? No, it's the Bible's thinking!

> For I am certain of this: neither death nor life, nor angels, nor princi-
> palities, nothing already in existence and nothing still to come, nor
> any power, nor the heights nor the depths, nor any created thing
> whatever, will be able to come between us and the love of God,
> known to us in Christ Jesus our Lord (Rom. 8:38–39, NJB).

> Therein lies the richness of God's free grace lavished upon us,
> imparting full wisdom and insight. He has made known to us his
> hidden purpose—such was his will and pleasure determined before-
> hand in Christ—to be put into effect when the time was ripe:
> namely, that the universe, all in heaven and on earth, might be
> brought into a unity in Christ (Eph. 1:7–10, NEB).

> Repent, therefore, and turn to God, so that your sins may be wiped
> out. Then the Lord may grant you a time of recovery and send the
> Messiah appointed for you, that is, Jesus. He must be received into
> heaven until the time comes for the universal restoration of which
> God has spoken through his holy prophets from the beginning (Acts
> 3:19–21, REB).

And here's one of the ways in which one of God's holy prophets, Isaiah, poetically described the time of the coming "universal restoration":

> The wolf shall dwell with the lamb,
>   and the leopard shall lie down with the kid . . .
>   and a little child shall lead them.
> The cow and the bear shall feed;
>   their young shall lie down together. . . .
> The sucking child shall play over the hole of the asp,
>   and the weaned child shall put his hand on the adder's den. . . .
> For the earth shall be full of the knowledge of the LORD
>   as the waters cover the sea.
>
> Isaiah 11:6–9

Wolves dwelling with lambs? Yes; in Isaiah's day just as in ours, wolves were a symbol of violent evil. And a little child, whom the church has always seen as Christ, shall lead them. And the "child shall put his hand on the adder's den." That is, there will be, through Christ, this "universal restoration" of all mankind from its original problem, the problem of sin, as symbolized by the serpent. Or as Paul put it, in terms of the garden of Eden, "As in Adam all men die, so in Christ all will be brought to life" (1 Cor. 15:22, NEB). And if "our Father who art in heaven" loves so much and desires such a reconciliation, doesn't it become us fathers and mothers (and all others) to follow in this attitude? We recall the words of Jesus: "There must be no limit to your goodness, as your heavenly Father's goodness knows no bounds" (Matt. 5:48, REB). Good grief! Who knows? There may even be beagles playing cards with the rabbits!

15. The God Who Took Away Our Sins

"All we like sheep have gone astray;
We have turned every one to his own way;
and the Lord has laid on him
the iniquity of us all."

Isaiah 53:6

The work of Jesus was basically revelatory: he came to *reveal*—to make known, to make us sure of—the Father and the Father's attitude toward us. And so Jesus could say, "I am the light of the world" (John 8:12, 9:5); "he who has seen me has seen the Father" (John 14:9); "O righteous Father, the world has not known thee, but I have known thee; and these know that thou hast sent me. I made known to them thy name, and I will make it known, that the love with which thou hast loved me may be in them, and I in them" (John 17:25–26); and so on. But what are the central ways in which Jesus reveals the Father to us? What are the most important ways in which this Christ-revealed knowledge about the Father is secured?

The New Testament sees everything it sees about Jesus "backward." That is, its entire view of Jesus is seen and understood from the perspective of his resurrection. For the earliest Christians the resurrection was the unmistakable outwardly visible seal or confirmation of *whom* they had been dealing with in Jesus. It was now no longer possible for them to see Jesus as merely another prophet or religious genius or charismatic personality or great political leader. In this man they had actually been dealing with God. That they had really been dealing with God's "only Son" is another way of saying the same thing. "I and the Father are one," as Jesus put it (John 10:30). It was primarily the resurrection that gave the first Christians the overwhelming certainty that Jesus was indeed the Christ, the long-awaited Messiah, God's once-and-for-all self-revelation of himself. So for this reason these people were, logically enough, called Christians.

But if the resurrection told the original Christians *who* Jesus was, what was there in the life of Jesus, more than any other

69

single thing, that told them *what* Jesus and/or God had revealed? Answer: the crucifixion. Because from the crucifixion they again looked backward, especially back to the prophet Isaiah.

In my estimation the most important single verse of scripture in the New Testament is Isaiah 53:6. That may sound strange, since Isaiah is an Old Testament book and Isaiah 53:6 is never quoted in so many words in the New Testament. But for some time in the earliest history of the church, the Old Testament was the only "scripture" this church had. And absolutely central to the faith of this church was the understanding of Christ's crucifixion as the fulfillment of Isaiah's prophecy: "All we like sheep have gone astray; we have turned every one to his own way; and the LORD has laid on him the iniquity of us all."

Notice the beautiful balance of this verse; it begins with "all" and ends with "all"—the all of our beginning and the all of our ending. And notice the way Paul maintains this balance in similar statements of his own, statements that no doubt have this prophecy of Isaiah in their background:

> For all alike have sinned, and are deprived of the divine glory; and all are justified by God's free grace alone, through his act of liberation in the person of Christ Jesus (Rom. 3:23–24, REB).

> As one man's trespass led to condemnation for all men, so one man's act of righteousness leads to acquittal and life for all men (Rom. 5:18).

> For God has consigned all men to disobedience, that he may have mercy upon all. . . . For from him and through him and to him are all things (Rom. 11:32, 36).

> As in Adam all die, so also in Christ shall all be made alive (1 Cor. 15:22).

There is also the same symmetrical correspondence to Isaiah's beginning and end when Jesus says:

> "Now is the judgment of this world; now the ruler of this world will be driven out. And I, when I am lifted up from the earth, will draw all people to myself." He said this to indicate the kind of death he was to die.
>
> John 12:31–32, NRSV

And what kind of death did Jesus die? It was a *kind* death for "all," just as Isaiah had foretold.

And so when the early Christians remembered the outstretched arms of Jesus on the cross, they knew those arms didn't mean a lack of knowledge like, for instance, the turned-up arms of an organ-pipe cactus; they knew those arms were meant to show the all-embracing love of God for his children—and all other creatures as well.

"*Now* is the judgment of this world," said Jesus before his crucifixion. That is, the future judgment, which we have for so long and so often incorrectly been told to fear, has already happened in the crucifixion. This entire world has been judged and has been found guilty. But in this amazing turnabout, worthy of the greatest joy and celebration, Jesus in his crucifixion has already borne this judgment for us: "and the Lord has laid on him the iniquity of us all."

In the "cruci-fix-ion," our knowledge of God's unconditional and conquering love for all of us is fixed—it's made clear once and for all; it's "nailed down"; it's secured. This is why Good Friday is good. And it's also why Paul can say:

> Through [Christ] God chose to reconcile the whole universe to himself, making peace through the shedding of his blood upon the cross—to reconcile all things, whether on earth or in heaven, through him alone (Col. 1:20, NEB).

And why John can say:

> My children, I am writing this to you so that you should not commit sin. But if anybody does, we have in Jesus Christ one who is acceptable to God and will plead our cause with the Father. He is himself a sacrifice to atone for our sins, and not ours only but the sins of the whole world (1 John 2:1–2, REB).

And why the writer of the letter to Hebrews can say:

> What we do see is Jesus, who for a short while was made subordinate to the angels, crowned now with glory and honour because he suffered death, so that, by God's gracious will, he should experience death for all mankind (Heb. 2:9, REB).

There is a French proverb that tells us, "To understand all is to forgive all." Regardless of who might have originally made this statement, the thought itself—like so many aspects of cultural wisdom—is easily traceable to the Bible. The psalmist, for instance, is quite certain of God's pardon and forgiveness:

> He pardons all my wrongdoing . . .
> and crowns me with love and compassion. . . .
> The LORD is compassionate and gracious,
> long-suffering and ever faithful;
> he will not always accuse
> or nurse his anger for ever.
> He has not treated us as our sins deserve
> or repaid us according to our misdeeds.
>   Psalm 103:3–4, 8–10, REB

And why is the Lord so compassionate? Because he understands. "For he knows how we were made, he remembers that we are but dust" (Ps. 103:14, REB).

When Jesus was crucified, he dramatized perfectly the forgiveness based on understanding when he said, "Father, forgive them; for they know not what they do" (Luke 23:34). Happily for us, then, God and/or Christ understands all of us much better than we could ever understand ourselves. And Solomon, in his God-given wisdom, also knew that to understand is to forgive.

But apart from Jesus' prayer of intercession when he was crucified, there is another sense in which his crucifixion includes his understanding of all of us: He takes up, he lifts, he bears, he literally "stands under" our sins, represented by the cross, and carries them away.

In our distress we often look for someone else who knows what it's like to feel like a fool, to be humiliated, disgraced, beaten, and degraded: someone who's been there, someone whose own arms have been outstretched with crucifixion. And usually such a person is not difficult to find.

But there is another who has gone through this experience precisely in order to lead us out of it. And this one is finally the only one strong enough to pick up, to stand under, and to carry away all our burdens for us. When we return to the Bible's mighty theme to see how it expresses this thought, it says, "Christ was innocent of sin, and yet for our sake God made him one with human sinfulness, so that in him we might be made one with the righteousness of God" (2 Cor. 5:21, REB). Or again, Isaiah 53:

> Surely he has borne our griefs
>   and carried our sorrows . . .
> he was wounded for our transgressions,
>   he was bruised for our iniquities;
> upon him was the chastisement that made us whole,
>   and with his stripes we are healed. . . .
> By his knowledge shall the righteous one, my servant,

make many to be accounted righteous;
and he shall bear their iniquities. . . .
He poured out his soul to death,
and was numbered with the transgressors;
yet he bore the sin of many,
and made intercession for the transgressors.

Isaiah 53:4–5, 11–12

In the crucifixion God has shown us clearly not only that he understands our sins but that he also stands under them and forgives them. When John the Baptist saw Jesus for the first time, he knew Jesus was the foretold Savior that everyone had been looking for—and is still looking for. And at that point John expressed very simply what is revealed to us in Jesus' crucifixion: "Behold, the Lamb of God, who takes away the sin of the world" (John 1:29).

16. Jesus, the One and Only Savior of the World

"All things have been delivered to me by my Father; and no one knows the Son except the Father, and no one knows the Father except the Son and any one to whom the Son chooses to reveal him."

—Matthew 11:27; Luke 10:22

Part of the earliest genius of the Jewish people was to long for, to search for, to passionately want to know the absolute truth—the *universally true.* They wanted to get to the rock bottom of things. Or, to put it in religious terms, they wanted to know God. Doesn't everyone? Sure, but this is an arduous quest that not everyone is up to.

The seriousness of this quest gave the Jews the ability to see that if they did find God, he would have to be the *only* God or else he wouldn't really *be* God. God, or "the Truth," must be universally true or else, by definition, it's not God or "the Truth"; it is only something partial, limited by something else. God must be true for all, or else he is not God at all. By definition, God is *one;* and therefore must be the "one-ly" or *only* God.

And so when the Jews did begin to find God (or, more accurately, when God began disclosing himself to the Jews), the first thing they were absolutely sure about was this: "Hear, O Israel: The LORD our God is one LORD" (Deut. 6:4; cf. Mark 12:29).

Thus Israel's entire relationship with God began with the commandment to remember that this God, just because he was

God, was the *only* God: "You shall have no other gods before me" (Deut. 5:7). Or, as one of the scribes said, agreeing with Jesus, "You are right, Teacher; you have truly said that [God] is one, and there is no other but he" (Mark 12:32). However, it wasn't long in Israel's history before the Jews began wanting to know more of God. God still seemed remote and rather tight-lipped, not giving his followers nearly as much to say about him as they would like to be able to say. "For God is in heaven, and you upon earth; therefore let your words be few," said Ecclesiastes, typical of Old Testament writers at this time, describing the remoteness of God (5:2). There were still many important things that needed to be cleared up.[18]

Consequently Israel's longing for God soon took on a new dimension. It wasn't that people began looking for a new God, but they developed the hope that the one and only God would remove the seemingly great distance between him and them. And finally an amazing expectation dawned: God would *show up*—personally, historically, in real flesh and blood. No longer would there be a great distance between God and his people, but God would come to his own and dwell among them (John 1:11, 14). No longer would there be an abstract, generalized, up-in-the-air, and rather impersonal quality about God. Now God would be concrete, particular, and specific, down-to-earth, a real flesh-and-blood human being. No longer would there be so much mystery surrounding God; now they could walk and talk with him, discuss things, get things clarified, even reach out and shake his hand if they wanted to.[19] "Oh, that I knew where I might find him!" Job said, expressing this passionate new hope and expectation in Israel (Job 23:3). In this person God would still be the one and only God, not another god or a second god. God would simply be *God*—who had come much closer: He'd be "the Messiah" or "the Christ." Or, if anyone had a hard time thinking of God and a person as being one and the same, he'd be God's "only Son" (John 3:16).

So they knew what they were looking for, and they waited. And because this was a *person* they were waiting for, they waited to learn this person's *name*. And so Israel's expectation of the Messiah worked very much like this:

This is why "the name of Jesus" has such significance through-out the New Testament. Not only does the meaning of this name reveal God's love and what God has already done: "You shall call his name Jesus, for he will save his people from their sins" (Matt. 1:21). But knowing this name would also now put people "in touch" with God in a way they'd never known before. Knowing this name, which identified this man, they now had a direct line to God. "For there is only one God, and there is only one media-tor between God and humanity, himself a human being, Christ Jesus" (1 Tim. 2:5, NJB). But Jesus was also "himself God." And so now the absolutely crucial link between God and man would be Jesus, the God-man. From now on, knowing this name, and the man it represented, would be like having God's home phone number. We would know where to find him; we could talk to him and hear what he had to say to us. Not knowing this name, and the person it represented, would be like looking for our one great love in all the wrong places, or constantly dialing numbers that result only in disappointing answers.

We often hear people talk about "the Word of God," by which they usually mean the Bible. But according to the Bible, the Word of God didn't become some 773,893 words. It didn't become ink and paper. "The Word became flesh and dwelt among us" (John 1:14). Strictly speaking, then, the one, single Word of God is the one, single name by which this one, single human individual is identified and characterized: *Jesus.*

For the earliest Christians this "onlyness" or exclusiveness of Jesus was an essential part of the good news. It meant they had "found the Messiah" (John 1:41). It meant that the one and only God—remote, distant, and abstract—had finally shown up as the one and only historical, concrete, flesh-and-blood God. But from the time this first happened, many people have been offended by this "onlyness" or exclusiveness. And so when Jesus first confessed to being "the one who is to come," he could also say, "and happy is he who does not find me an obstacle to faith" (Luke 7:19, 23, REB). Isaiah had prophesied that many would trip over this "foundation stone" (Isa. 28:16; Rom. 9:33). In this world a clear assertion about anything is going to be contradicted. But we can especially expect many people to be stopped dead in their tracks if they hear something like this:

> This Jesus is "the stone that was rejected by you, the builders; it has become the cornerstone." There is salvation in no one else, for there is no other name under heaven given among mortals by which we must be saved.
>
> Acts 4:11–12, NRSV

Jesus is "the Savior of the world" (John 4:42, 1 John 4:14)— the *whole* world. He is the Savior who "desires all men to be saved and to come to the knowledge of the truth" (1 Tim. 2:4). And so all men and women will. But in the meantime how do we know this is true? Only through faith in Jesus. As Karl Barth has put it:

> These two things must be carefully considered: the uniqueness of Christ and his significance for the whole world, the concentration and the universality of grace. It is *here* that grace is found, in Jesus Christ: but it is grace intended for the whole world, since it is grace.[20]

And so Jesus is *the one and only Savior of the world.* He is the necessary, particular first step to this total, universal reconciliation, the step on the basis of which this reconciliation actually begins happening in people's lives right now. But of course it's always the first step of any reconciliation that's the hardest.

Ultimately Christian faith is anchored (Heb. 6:19), "rooted and grounded" (Eph. 3:17) in the historical person of Jesus of Nazareth and *who he was*. Without Jesus being *who* he was—that is, the one and only God or Son of God—*what* Jesus said and did, all of the life and work of Jesus, of Christians, and of the churches, is finally groundless, rootless, without foundation, without staying power or authority. Without this firm historical anchor of the incarnation, that actually *"God was in Christ* reconciling the world to himself," then Christian faith and all of its reconciling activity will just as easily be blown away and disappear as Woodstock without his anchor—anchors (following Hebrews 6:19) being a traditional symbol for Jesus.

When people run up against this hard historical core of Christian faith, the incarnation of God in Christ, there are of course several ways they can react. They can renounce Christian faith altogether. Or if for some reason they want to apply the word "Christian" to whatever faith they do have, they can reinterpret the meaning of Christian faith by simply watering down its essence in the divinity of Jesus. In subtle or not-so-subtle ways, they use Jesus as a mere symbol, a personification, or "the best example" for whatever their center of value actually is. This is the ancient heresy of docetism: Jesus the historical person only *seems* to be the object of faith.

But what causes people to be stopped by Jesus, the living "stone [we] trip over, a rock [we] stumble against"? (1 Peter 2:8, REB). In my opinion it's usually because these folks haven't yet been driven to a deep enough *need* for God. If and when people's need for God becomes consciously serious enough, they'll be able to see with the clarity of desperation that God, if he really is God, must be the one and only God. This need will also force them, like the Jews of old, to hope that God will show up as a single, historical "flesh-and-blood" individual who will come among us and love us—and yet this individual will remain the one and only God. Only when the need is deep enough can the stumbling stone become the foundation stone. Only when one is hungry and thirsty enough can one *really*, in this sense, swallow the flesh and blood of Jesus, as Jesus said we must (John 6:53–56).

Christian faith is simply the faith that believes at the depth of the human heart that Jesus is this God—that "Jesus is the Christ" (see Matt. 16:16; John 11:27; Acts 5:42) is another way to say the same thing. No one is forced to believe this. How could any human power force this belief on another person anyway? But if we don't believe at least this, surely there's no logic in calling our faith "Christian." For ultimately we'd be worshiping something else. Finally our faith would be something other than a Jesus-secured or Christ-centered faith. So—why call it "Christian"?

17. The Spirit of Love and How We Come to Know It

"Jesus replied, 'The teaching that I give is not my own; it is the teaching of him who sent me. Whoever has the will to do the will of God shall know whether my teaching comes from him or is merely my own.' "

—John 7:16–17, NEB

Dostoevsky tells us that "hell is the suffering of being unable to love."[21] But on the other hand, if we define hell as the absolute "nothing worse," Charlie Brown would argue that hell is "being unloved"—or, in any case, *feeling* unloved, since this is obviously how Charlie Brown feels. "There's nothing worse than being unloved," he contends, no matter what Lucy or Dostoevsky might say.

Basically, at heart, everyone is looking for love. And because "God is love" (1 John 4:8, 16), this is just another way of saying everyone is looking for God. Augustine was being completely true to one of the Bible's most basic beliefs when he formulated this belief by saying, "Our hearts are formed for thee, O Lord, and are restless until they find their rest in thee."

This is what the Bible's teaching of "original sin" has always meant to convey: that our hearts always originate, start out, "are formed" for God, but our hearts will remain empty, restless, unsatisfied until God, coming from outside in, fills them with his own loving presence. We do not have within ourselves—or begin life with—what we basically need to fulfill ourselves. Only God himself, who comes from outside ourselves, can do that. No one else and nothing else can put in what God has left out.

And so Paul, speaking of all people, can say, "I know of nothing good living in me—in my natural self, that is—for though the will to do what is good is in me, the power to do it is not" (Rom. 7:18, NJB).

The last gospels anyone will ever hear the Bible preaching are the gospels of *self*-esteem and *self*-confidence and *self*-actualization. These will always be attractive and touching human dreams. But the Bible is being supremely realistic about human nature when it constantly asserts that the love and esteem and confidence and actualization we all yearn for must finally come from God and not from us. Or, as another one of my theological heroes, Dietrich Bonhoeffer, can say about this human situation as it relates to the Bible's mighty theme:

> That God loved the world and reconciled it to himself in Christ is the central message proclaimed in the New Testament. It is assumed there that the world stands in need of reconciliation with God but that it is not capable of achieving it by itself.[22]

In a situation like this, we'll always wish we could be God ourselves. But there's no way!

How does this situation of ours work itself out in actual practice? In the practice of idolatry—or "sin." And what is an idol—or sin? From the Christian perspective, an idol (or sin) is indicated precisely by the word "Christian" itself: It is when a person's center of value is anything or anyone other than Christ himself. An idol is anything other than Christ with which we try to satisfy our God-hungry hearts. Whether we think of this basic and original emptiness as loneliness or the need for love or a sort of vague spiritual thirst or whatever, Christian faith claims only Christ can cure it or fill it up. Christ himself is just that key which alone can fit and open the closed locks of our hearts. Anything else is an idol and finally won't fill the emptiness.

But most often this false center of value is another self—ourselves. And what is the result of idolatry? The result of idolatry—or "the wages of sin"—is death (Rom. 6:23). And this means a *living* death or "hell," trying to live without God living inside us in the person of God's (and/or Christ's) Holy Spirit.

Love seeks closeness. And so it was that when the people of Israel began yearning for the Messiah to come, they were actually longing for God himself, for love, to draw closer, to come out of the clouds and to become flesh, to become a real, living historical human being. And so God, love, the Word, "became flesh and dwelt among us" in the particular man Jesus (John 1:14). This is why Jesus was also called "Immanuel"—that is, "God is with us" (Isa. 7:14).

God was with us, but then he left. That is, God in the person of Jesus left. And "even if we were once familiar with Christ according to human standards, we do not know him in that way any longer," as Paul could say (2 Cor. 5:16, NJB). So after the time of God's visiting us in Jesus, our question to God then becomes, "Where do we go from here?"

And now the good news is that God the Father, through his Son, has drawn even closer to us—as close as it's possible to come. He now comes to us—*in* us—in the person of his Spirit. Again, God has not become a new god or a third god. God has simply completely closed the gap between himself and us. God the heavenly Father became God the down-to-earth historical Son through whom we can now know God's own heart-fulfilling Spirit. And in case anyone might not have recognized it, this is what is called "the Holy Trinity." The Trinity is simply God's own three-point route for overcoming the lack of real understanding between him and humankind, a lack of understanding far worse than even any of the following:

The Spirit of God is something no one should ever try to live without. As a matter of fact, from the biblical standpoint anyone without the Spirit of God isn't *really living!* And so Jesus could say to the man who wanted to go and bury his father before following Jesus, "Follow me, and leave the dead to bury their own dead" (Matt. 8:22). On the other hand, "the fruit of the Spirit is love, joy, peace, patience, kindness, goodness, faithfulness, gentleness, self-control" (Gal. 5:22–23). Who would want to live without that? So the question now becomes: How do we come to know this Spirit?

The answer is simple. It's found in two words of Jesus we just quoted: "Follow me!" This is what it means to believe in Jesus. It means to obey him. What's the command? Again, very simple: that we "cease to live for [ourselves]. . . . " and instead "live for him" (2 Cor. 5:15, REB). And what does this mean? It means, as we said before, to live for the single purpose of making known the love of God made known through Christ. The lives of all of us witness to or point to whatever our central value or ultimate concern happens to be, whether this value or concern is ourselves or something or someone outside ourselves. The Christian is a person whose life is primarily an ongoing conscious attempt to point to Christ as the universally true and needed central value or concern. Again, this is why Christians are called "Christians." The entire work of the Christian man or woman, said Martin Luther, can be summarized this way: "To this man [Christ] thou shalt point and say, 'Here is God.' "[23] So, then, who or what we follow, obey, or believe in finally comes down to Charlie Brown's question: Who am I pointing to?

When our lives point to Christ, when in this sense we "follow Christ," then something will happen to us. Not before. The Spirit of God will come into us and confirm this first step we've taken. First, "Come to me"; then, "I will give you rest" (Matt. 11:28). The joy, the Spirit, is actually *in the obedience, in the giving*.

Of course the first time we take this step, it's really a leap of faith. Because how can we initially witness to a Spirit of love that comes to us only as a result, a by-product, of our witnessing? In this case, you "Assume a virtue if you have it not," to use Shakespeare's words (*Hamlet,* III.IV.160). That is, we assume this message is true and we *act* on it. As Jesus could say, "If you know this, happy are you if you act upon it" (John 13:17, NEB). Because after this first action, there should then be the birth and beginning growth of a real *heartfelt* knowledge and conviction behind our witnessing to God's love. Of course what we're trying to say here has already been said infinitely better by Jesus:

> Anyone who has received my commands and obeys them—he it is who loves me; and he who loves me will be loved by my Father; and I will love him and disclose myself to him. . . . Anyone who loves me will heed what I say; then my Father will love him, and we will come to him and make our dwelling with him.
>
> John 14:21, 23, REB

First the obedience; then the disclosing, which comes from the indwelling.

In short, Christian faith believes that all people are born—or "originate"—with a deep, built-in hunger spot that only Christ can fill. This is what it means to be created in the image of God (Gen. 1:27); it means to be created with God's own Christ-shaped, "made-for-Christ," but hollow, image in us. Therefore, the basic task of every Christian is simply to "hit the spot" with Christ. And it's finally in this very work of attempting to hit the spot in others that Christians experience their own spots being hit. So how would we define Christ, "the image of the invisible God" (Col. 1:15), in this scheme of things? He is the one and only "night cookie" that can really hit the spot and can really fill the night with light.

18. The Bible and Five Types of Freedom

"You must work out your own salvation in fear and trembling; for it is God who works in you, inspiring both the will and the deed, for his own chosen purpose."

—Philippians 2:12-13, NEB

"May I say that all too often men are betrayed by the word 'freedom'?"[24] Boy, did Kafka know what he was talking about when he made that statement! And just as it was true in Kafka's day, so was it also true in the time of Jesus and Paul. And it's also true today. This is too bad, because for the Bible "freedom" is a key concept. The idea of freedom, in one form or another, saturates the Bible's pages. The Bible is the book of freedom par excellence. It's based on freedom and it produces freedom. Consequently, the entire Bible, especially the New Testament, goes to great lengths to explain exactly what it means and doesn't mean by freedom. But still we're all too often betrayed by this word. So I hope I'll be forgiven for taking one more run at it.

I see five different types of freedom being discussed by the Bible, and it seems to me that all five are touched on by Paul in the brief passage from Philippians just quoted. So here we go!

Spiritual Freedom. When Paul uses the word "salvation" here, he's pointing to one type of freedom—spiritual freedom. This is because salvation basically means that something is "made safe" or free from harm or danger. So when Paul advises Christians to "accept salvation as your helmet" (Eph. 6:17, REB), he's telling them that in Christ they'll be safe or free from all spiritual harm or danger. They'll be safe or free from the hardest spiritual blows that anyone or anything can throw at them—even if it's spiritual beanballs.

Spiritual freedom can be either a present or a future reality. *Present* spiritual freedom means freedom from the here-and-now crushing bondage to sin. ",Where the Spirit of the Lord is," says Paul, "there is freedom" (2 Cor. 3:17); and that means "to be free from anxious care" (1 Cor. 7:32, REB); it means freedom from the unhappiness that invariably results from being addicted to sin. Again, sin means worshiping false gods. False gods are false lovers; they initially hold out a lot of hope and promise but only force us into an unhappy slavery in which we aren't really ourselves, and then they finally disappoint us for good.

But salvation or spiritual freedom can also refer to a *future* reality in which we will ultimately be safe or free, not only from sin but also from death and all the other evils of this life. And so in the following statement Paul can refer to spiritual freedom or salvation in both their present and future senses: "But now that you have been set free from sin and have become slaves of God, the return you get is sanctification and its end, eternal life" (Rom. 6:22). So being a "slave of God" is freedom, the very best for our spirits, in this life and in the life to come!

The Dreadful Freedom.[25]   Paul is alluding to this type of freedom when he says, "Work out your own salvation *in fear and trembling.*" Christian faith assumes all people begin their lives as sinners or idolators. Again, this is what is meant by "original sin." The idea may not appeal to us, but to deny it is also to deny Christ. For the less the problem of sin is taken seriously, the less Christ, the savior from sin, will be taken seriously. "Here are words you may trust, words that merit full acceptance: 'Christ Jesus came into the world to save sinners' " (1 Tim. 1:15, NEB). A shallow view of sin is only one side of the coin; the other side is always a shallow view of Christ.

And so faith in Christ tells us that originally all of us have faith in something else. And this in turn means that this "something else," whatever it might be, must first completely fail us before we'll ever be desperate enough to grab hold of something radically new. When people really worship something, they're not going to give up that something until they have to. Why should they? And if they should have to, where are they going to find something else to take that false god's place?

When this experience happens to us—that is, the complete collapse of all our old, original gods—this means longer or shorter periods of time in our lives when we have nothing to hang on to. This is "fear and trembling." It is "free" because we are free of anything to cling to, and it's "dreadful" for the same reason. For a longer or shorter period of time, we have no faith in *anything*; there is no deeper human suffering. Its depth comes precisely from the fact that there's no bottom to this suffering. It's a free fall in which one never gets to the bottom of things or comes to rest on anything firm or substantial. There are no satisfying answers but only radically unanswerable questions. And if

the effects of this kind of suffering are difficult to watch, we
should consider those who are actually going through it.

Nevertheless, this spiritual death is the doorway through
which the New Testament claims all idolatrous faith must pass
in order to find faith in Christ and, in him, an altogether substantial newness of life. This is the death that always precedes
being "born again" (John 3:3, REB).

Because this suffering has a supernatural and not a natural
basis, it will usually leave the "science" of psychology scratching
its head. Apart from Christians, about the only people who
would seem to have any understanding of it at all are artists and
literary folk, whose sensitivity often forces them to witness to
this dimension of the infinite in each individual. But for the
Bible, this experience, represented chiefly by baptism and the
cross, is an essential component of its witness. There is absolutely no way of understanding the New Testament's message
without at least *intellectually* understanding this experience.

The very first of Jesus' beatitudes is this: "Blessed are the poor in spirit, for theirs is the kingdom of heaven" (Matt. 5:3). This is a paradox the Bible is constantly admonishing us to learn—that only the lowly, the meek, the humble, the sorrowful, the "poor in spirit" can find and know God.

For the New Testament, baptism and the cross are not just the baptism and cross of Jesus, although they are certainly that. Baptism and the cross are also symbols for the spiritual death that must initiate everyone who follows Jesus. Paul puts it this way:

> You cannot have forgotten that all of us, when we were baptised into Christ Jesus, were baptised into his death. So by our baptism into his death we were buried with him, so that as Christ was raised from

the dead by the Father's glorious power, we too should begin living a
new life.

Romans 6:3–4, NJB

It's this view of baptism, by the way, that has caused many
Christians, including me, to feel that baptizing by "sprinkling
little babies" is an inappropriate symbol for what's being symbolized.[26] The "new life" spoken of here is not the one little
babies are beginning. Paul continues:

> Our former self was crucified with him, so that the self which be-
> longed to sin should be destroyed and we should be freed from the
> slavery of sin. . . . In the same way, you must see yourselves as be-
> ing dead to sin but alive for God in Christ Jesus.
>
> Romans 6:6, 11, NJB

So, for Christians, "new life" is always found through this
death of the old self; spiritual freedom is found only by passing
through the experience of "the dreadful freedom," the experience of "fear and trembling." To follow Christ we must be crucified with him, which always means the failure and death of our
old gods. And to be crucified, as the New Testament sometimes
defines the word, is to be hanged on a tree (Acts 5:30; 10:39).

The freedom of the crucified heart, the dreadful freedom of having nothing at all to give us security or to comfort us, is the freedom that forces us to find spiritual freedom, the joyful freedom we come to know in obedience to Christ. When we first become acquainted with spiritual freedom, it's a revolutionary experience unlike anything we've ever known in depth and intensity. It's revolutionary because it's like being suddenly turned around or set right side up. Thus the New Testament speaks of this experience as "conversion" or "justification": that is, being made "just" or "right" or "just right" in our attitude toward God.

But this dramatic prologue at the beginning of Christian life is also the pattern for a learning process that will then continue. And this is because, being the sinful creatures we are, we always tend to forget ourselves, and over and over again we find ourselves serving false gods. We stray. But then we're jerked back onto the path of obedience by once more experiencing the dreadful freedom that always results from idolatry. And so Christian life always involves the attempt to "make holiness perfect in the fear of God" (2 Cor. 7:1). As a matter of fact, Christians come to look upon their own grief as good (oh, good grief!) because they learn to appreciate the essential role grief plays in keeping them on the "strait . . . and narrow" (Matt. 7:14, KJV). Indeed, like Paul, they "will all the more gladly boast of [their] weaknesses" since they have learned that God's "power is made perfect in weakness" (2 Cor. 12:9).

This process of learning by the alternating current of dreadful freedom/spiritual freedom is called "sanctification" by the New Testament. "Justification" is like getting signed up for a course that's just what we need, and "sanctification" is like actually taking this course. And the course itself is called "remedial living," because it's learning how to *really* live by following Christ. Christ "is just. He is himself the remedy for the defilement of our sins, not our sins only but the sins of all the world" (1 John 2:2, NEB).

Freedom of Choice or Political Freedom. Freedom of choice is the opportunity to choose what we like. It's an ice-cream shop with fifty different flavors. It's the freedom to go into business with such an ice-cream shop. It's a secret voting booth with lots of different candidates to choose from. It's a system of government that allows the greatest possible freedom for individuals to think, say, write, read, worship, and pursue what they please. This is freedom of choice, and the Bible provides a strong foundation for this type of freedom primarily in six ways.

First, freedom of choice is supported by the Bible's highest of all possible regard for individual men and women as God's children. We have already noted how Christ "sacrificed himself to win freedom for all mankind" (1 Tim. 2:6, NEB). This of course includes even the person most "insignificant" or "lost" by human standards. And thus Jesus could say, "Truly I tell you:

anything you did for one of my brothers here, however insignificant, you did for me" (Matt. 25:40, REB). The church is God's "missing persons" bureau, and its constitution is the Bible. Therefore it's not possible for such a Bible-constituted people to even think of a person who isn't "much of a person" or who isn't loved infinitely by God.

Any group of people deeply influenced by the Bible is going to have the Bible's own high regard for individual human beings and therefore is going to do everything it can to increase people's freedom of choice. This is because this kind of freedom is so basic to what it means to be human that to deprive people of it is like taking away a bird's ability to fly. Our ability to choose is a gift given by God especially to humankind. And so when anyone is denied the opportunity to exercise this ability, by governments or others who want to be too controlling, it is a sad, dehumanizing business indeed.

Second, freedom of choice is supported by the biblical view of human nature. For even though the Bible knows people to be infinitely loved by God, it also knows them to be sinners. It knows that God's children all have a deep, built-in selfish streak; they possess an extremely strong tendency to shove other people aside in order to get what they want. And it's precisely for this reason that some of the greatest advocates of freedom of choice or political freedom have been those Christians who have taken most seriously the Bible's insistent emphasis on humankind's sinful nature. John Calvin, for instance, was certainly a theologian noted for his strong views on the strength of human selfishness. And it was exactly this view that finally made Calvinism one of the greatest forces for political freedom in the modern world. As Calvin could say in 1559:

The vice or imperfection of men therefore renders it safer and more tolerable for the government to be in the hands of many, that they may afford each other mutual assistance and admonition, and that if any one arrogate to himself more than is right, the many may act as censors and masters to restrain his ambition.[27]

It was in this same wise tradition that a latter-day Calvinist, Abraham Lincoln, probably the United States' greatest president as well as her greatest theologian, could say, "No man is good enough to govern another man, without that other's consent."[28] Lincoln, who knew the Bible as well as most ministers, was also fond of quoting Jeremiah 17:9: "The heart is deceitful above all things, and desperately corrupt; who can understand it?"

Well, in answer to Jeremiah's question, Lincoln had a pretty good understanding of the human heart. But Lucy doesn't. And therefore giving people freedom of choice (like letting Linus worship his blanket if he wants to) will probably never be one of her great strengths:

Third, the Bible supports freedom of choice by its emphasis on—and its understanding of—faith. Back to Paul's statement: "You must work out your own salvation." If you haven't done this yourself, it's not your faith or your salvation. In order for faith to be faith, we must arrive at it ourselves. Therefore the Bible will always be an extremely strong force for creating societies and governments where this kind of individual "working out" is allowed to take place without interference.

Fourth, the Bible produces freedom of choice because it's susceptible to a wide variety of interpretations, and therefore "independent thinking" and diversity of opinion will always increase wherever people are allowed to read it and they *do* read it. And this type of thinking, where people are thus encouraged to think for themselves, will always make a lot of difficulties for all dictatorial governments and churches. This is one reason why there is usually a striking correlation between countries with strong democracies and a wide variety of groups within these countries who read the Bible.[29]

Fifth, the Bible produces freedom of choice by providing people with a basis for meaning, morality, and unselfishness. When these things are strong in a society, there can be more freedom. The population is not driven into so much desperate viciousness and selfishness by the lack of meaning in life. But when people *are* desperately vicious and selfish, more and more law is required, until finally we find ourselves living in a police state or an armed camp. When people no longer believe in God and an "eternal life" after this one, they'll only find their hope in this life and therefore will be desperate to get from life everything they can while they can. If we only go around once and that's it, we'll eventually find ourselves greedily grabbing all the gusto we can before it's too late. Sally Brown decided one Christmas to be unselfish by not asking for any presents.[30] But by ignoring the true present of Christmas, Christ, this is the conclusion she finally came to:

Without the Bible's basis for meaning, morality, and unselfishness, we all tend to move in this same direction. And this always bodes ill for our freedom of choice. The Bible tells us that "as lawlessness spreads, the love of many will grow cold" (Matt. 24:12, REB). But it's also true that, as love grows cold, lawlessness will spread. Without belief in the God of love, life truly becomes this vicious cycle.

Sixth, the Bible produces more freedom of choice because it tends to create an educated and literate people, and such a people will always be more difficult to enslave by church or state or both. For instance, public education grew largely out of the Protestant Reformation. The Reformers wanted people to be educated precisely in order that they could read the Bible for themselves, make their own intelligent decisions about its meaning, and no longer be forced into deadly spiritual straitjackets. This is why, when we can read the Bible but don't, we're just as vulnerable to fitting into a mindless slavery as those who *can't* read it.

And so it's amazing but true: More than anything else in the world, it is the Bible that has steadily pushed humankind toward greater and greater freedom of choice or political freedom. This is why all political and spiritual tyrants have always feared the Bible and have tried to keep it either under wraps or tightly under control. They can see that both political freedom and spiritual freedom are produced by the Bible.

All of this may sound very hopeful. And so at the same time we need to be fully aware of this disturbing paradox: The more freedom of choice we have, a freedom that's ultimately derived from the Bible, the less we seem to be using this freedom for reading and knowing the Bible. And of course when freedom of choice is cut away from its source like this, it stands an excellent chance of withering and dying. When the foundation begins to go, the superstructure can't be far behind. This is what now seems to be happening. And it results in the depressing situation in which the highest meaning of the word "free" is that something doesn't cost any money.

Jesus tells us, "If you dwell within the revelation I have brought, you are indeed my disciples; you shall know the truth, and the truth will set you free" (John 8:31–32, NEB). No doubt we are justified in interpreting the word "free" here in both a spiritual and political sense—precisely in the order of first the spiritual, then the political, just as Jesus was speaking here in primarily a spiritual sense. But before we can have either of these, we must first be his disciples. "If then the Son sets you free, you will indeed be free" (John 8:36, NEB).

Freedom of the Will or "Free Will." Freedom of choice is when we can choose what we like; "free will" says we can also choose to like it. No one has this kind of freedom. No one decides to fall in love. I can walk into the "fifty different flavors" shop and choose what I like. But I always choose the same thing: chocolate. I don't choose to like chocolate. I've got to have it. There's something in my biological makeup that causes me to crave it. And I am no more free to give up my love for chocolate than Linus is free to renounce his devotion to the Great Pumpkin.

In other words, "free will" claims there are no causes outside of a person's own will that make people do what they do. It says that if a person does something, they have only themselves to blame—or to thank. It says that our wills are finally operating outside of the realm of causality.

This view makes a mockery of two things. First is nature. Says Kafka of this type of "freedom": " 'Human freedom,' I thought. 'Self-controlled movement.' What a mockery of holy Mother Nature!"[31] What a mockery of nature's laws to say that those laws are in effect everywhere except in the area of the human will, that the will is "free" from the natural laws of cause and effect, that nothing *causes* our wills to choose what they choose. Try to talk any scientist into this view of "freedom," and he or she will laugh loud and long. "What a mockery of holy Mother Nature" indeed!

But "free will" also makes a mockery of the Bible and of God. The Bible quite obviously assumes that people often have freedom of choice: "You must work out your own salvation," to go back to Paul's statement. But do *we* finally do the choosing? Are *our wills* finally "free" or in charge? Paul's statement here is typical of the entire Bible's view on who does the choosing: "Work out your own salvation . . . *for it is God who works in you, inspiring both the will and the deed, for his own chosen purpose.*" The entire Bible is extremely clear on this point. It nowhere says that people have "free will," but emphatically says just the opposite. For instance, Paul, quoting the Old Testament, tells us:

> [God] says to Moses, "I will show mercy to whom I will show mercy, and have pity on whom I will have pity." Thus it does not depend on human will or effort, but on God's mercy. . . . Thus he not only shows mercy as he chooses, but also makes stubborn as he chooses.
>
> Romans 9:15–16, 18, REB

The Bible is very consistent. It tells us that what is always and totally in control is *God*'s choice, *God*'s will, *God*'s power, *God*'s election, *God*'s sovereignty, *God*'s providence, *God*'s plan, *God*'s grace, and *God*'s predestining. If God is God, *God* is in charge.

But doesn't this also tell us exactly why the idea of "free will" had to be fought so strenuously when the Bible was written and still has to be fought in the same way today? Because if we have "free will," this means *we* are in charge. And if *we* are in charge, then *we* are our own god! Just what we've always wanted! This is human pride or sinfulness traced to its very root—"and you will be like God" (Gen. 3:5, RSV). "For *thine* is the . . . power" (emphasis added) the Lord's prayer teaches us (Matt. 6:13, KJV). But it's just not the nature of us men and women to want it this way.

Make no mistake. To say that we have this kind of freedom, the freedom of "free will," is to say that finally we ourselves are gods; and of course the reason we will always want to say this is our own titanic pride in ourselves. It is precisely sin, or people's own basic worship of themselves, that will always cause "free will" to be an extremely popular but shallow way of viewing things. And it's also because this imaginary freedom is sin that the Bible steadfastly denies all salvation by "works," or "merit," or self-righteousness, or "free will." All people, including Christians, will always have a natural-born desire to be their own gods, and "free will" is the last and most subtle refuge for this basic and idolatrous desire. "Free will" is finally a kind of "hidden humanism," or denial that God really is God. "Free will" is a euphemism for self-righteousness; it is the last holdout or hiding place for self-worship. And self-worship is the childhood dream that's the last thing we want to part with.

"But, ah!" you say. "This is very clever of you, Mr. Short! When you do something good or right for once in your life, you can humbly give God the credit, and this will be very commendable of you. But also, when you do something bad or wrong (where you really shine!), you can do the same thing, give God the credit and claim, 'It's not my fault! There were forces acting on me over which I have no control! I was merely a passive victim! Sob! Sniff!' Very clever of you, Mr. Short!"

What's to prevent Christians from practicing this kind of subterfuge or self-deception? How does one hold together Christian obedience to God along with *God*'s power, predestination, and sovereignty? How is it possible to *live* as if it all depends on us (as faith lives), if we really *believe* it all depends on God (as faith believes)?

Answer: These two essential things are held together by the clear-minded knowledge, which comes from excruciating experience, that this subterfuge *doesn't work*. The living experiences of faith and lack of faith teach us—quite vividly, right here and now—that no one gets away with anything. For instance, the Old Testament knows nothing of a punishment or judgment in some future life; all the punishments and judgments that the Old Testament talks about (and it talks about plenty of them) are punishments and judgments that take place here and now in *this* life. And yet the Old Testament tells us, "Be assured, the wicked will not go unpunished" (Prov. 11:21, NRSV). The unvarying law is this: When we disobey God, regardless of whose fault it may be, we catch hell for it. This is precisely what "hell" is. "The wages of sin *is* death"—present tense, present reality (Rom. 6:23). When people really learn, from personal experience, that this strict spiritual law of gravity really is true and in constant operation, then they'll not be at all interested in practicing disobedience and blaming it on God. And at the same time they'll learn that taking credit for their obedience (which "free will" gives them) is just another form of disobedience. All of this may seem tremendously unfair since God himself is completely in charge of the whole operation. But there comes a point when one quits quibbling about what's fair or unfair and learns—for one's own good—to obey. This is why the Old Testament can also tell us, "The fear of the LORD is the beginning of wisdom" (Prov. 9:10). Later, it seems to me, it's gratitude as much as any other motive that produces Christian obedience. But initially, like rowdy, unruly children, we're taught to obey out of fear. At the beginning of their journey, Christians, just like Linus here, are "saved by a gentle reminder"—albeit a much more dangerous *spiritual* reminder.

"Free will" is part of the law. When we think we have this imaginary freedom, our relationship to God will always be a legal relationship. "If I do this, then God will do that." And in this way we control God. Just as we said of the law in Meditation 13, "free will" likewise always tells us, "It's up to you!" But real freedom comes to us only from obedience to God *by God's grace*—that is, by *his* love and *his* power. If it is not by God's power, it is not freedom, it is not obedience, and it is not grace. Or, as Paul can say:

> For freedom Christ has set us free. Stand firm, therefore, and do not submit again to a yoke of slavery. . . . You who want to be justified by the law have cut yourselves off from Christ; you have fallen away from grace.
>
> Galatians 5:1, 4, NRSV

We can no more decide to be Christians on the basis of our own wills than we can decide to be cacti or orange trees. We are *made* cacti or Christians or orange trees. Cacti, Christians, and orange trees are God's creation, not our own. And so not being "self-made" (as we would surely like to be), we really don't have all that much to say about our own marvelous "decision."

Christians know that all things obey God totally out of conscious or unconscious necessity, and that they themselves obey totally out of conscious *emotional* necessity. If their obedience were not totally necessary, they could, just to this decisive extent, be proud of themselves and have something to boast of. But

> by grace you have been saved through faith, and this is not your own doing; it is the gift of God—not the result of works, so that no one may boast. For we are what he has made us, created in Christ Jesus for good works, which God prepared beforehand to be our way of life.
>
> Ephesians 2:8–10, NRSV

Or, as the Bible's mighty theme (2 Cor. 5:18–21, REB) begins by saying, "All this has been the work of God"!

Freedom from Deified Law. We can choose what we want or will or like (that means we can have free choice), but we can't choose to want or will or like it (that means we don't have "free will"). When our wants or wills are finally brought into conformity with God's will, "it is God working in you, inspiring both the will and the deed, for his own chosen purpose" (Phil. 2:13, REB). When our wills are finally bent to doing God's will, it is *God* who has made this choice and changed our wills, not us.

It's the law that tells us that our salvation is up to us; "The man who does this shall gain life by it" (Rom. 10:5, NEB). But being our own saviors is a responsibility that either crushes us with its burden or infatuates us with self-righteousness. And so Paul can finally say of this law that promised life, "The commandment came . . . and I died" (Rom. 7:9).

In the New Testament's view, the law can either deify us or it can deify itself. That is, the law not only can beguile us about the power and freedom of our own *wills,* duping us into thinking we can save ourselves and thus can be our own lords and saviors, but the law can also mislead us by telling us there is a divine "written code" of *deeds* we can do that will always save us. Of course, in this case Christ is no longer the savior, the written code is. When this kind of law has ultimate authority over us, there is only bondage in it and never freedom. Thus Paul can say, primarily to converts from Judaism:

> So too, my friends, through the body of Christ you died to the law and were set free to give yourselves to another, to him who rose from the dead so that we may bear fruit for God. . . . Now, having died to that which held us bound, we are released from the law, to serve God in a new way, the way of the spirit in contrast to the old way of a written code.
>
> Romans 7:4, 6, REB

And what's this "old way of a written code"? It can be any prescribed list of do's and don'ts, but here it refers to the Old Testament's law of Moses, that vast maze of "Thou shall's" and "Thou shall not's," which will always become so complex and constraining and hairsplitting that one could easily starve to death before one learns what thou shall not do next.

The New Testament's attitude toward the Mosaic law is that it's good but it isn't God. It isn't Lord. "Jesus is Lord" (Rom. 10:9; 1 Cor. 12:3). And thus Jesus is expressing the New Testament's view of the law as a whole when he says of part of it— namely, Sabbath observance—"The sabbath was made for man, not man for the sabbath; so the Son of man is lord even of the sabbath" (Mark 2:27–28; "the Son of man" refers to Jesus).

But if there's no absolute code of law or ethics for the Christian to follow, exactly what is it that the Christian is called to *do?* When God, working in us, inspires both the will and the deed for God's own chosen purpose, just what is this deed and what is this purpose? Again, the answer is such a single deed and single purpose that we can hardly believe it: We're to make known the love of God made known through Christ. But aren't

there some laws or rules or regulations to act as infallible guides
for achieving this deed and purpose? No! Finally there aren't.
We're free. We're free to use our own critical intelligence, our
own creativity and imagination. If there were finally such an
absolutized set of guidelines, we'd again be "under the law."
And "those who rely on obedience to the law are under a curse
. . . Christ bought us freedom from the curse of the law" (Gal.
3:10, 13, REB). So living under the law is living under a curse.
On the other hand, if we live "under Christ," we know that a
curse will always dog all laws that don't serve him.[32]

"If we are in union with Christ Jesus circumcision makes no
difference at all, nor does the want of it; the only thing that
counts is faith active in love" (Gal. 5:6, NEB). In every word and
deed, in every action of our lives, we're to express this faith,

we're to "speak out" and to say or to show what we do know. As Paul puts it:

> But Scripture says, "I believed, and therefore I spoke out," and we too, in the same spirit of faith, believe and therefore speak out; for we know that he who raised the Lord Jesus to life will with Jesus raise us too, and bring us to his presence, and you with us.
>
> 2 Corinthians 4:13–14, NEB

Talk about good news! Talk about something that can help and make a difference! The purpose of the church and the purpose of every Christian is simply to "spread the Word." We've been given the light; we're to let it shine and pass it on. Said Jesus, "Let your light so shine before men, that they may see your good works and give glory to your Father who is in heaven" (Matt. 5:16). Or, as the Bible's mighty theme puts it, "God . . . has entrusted us with the message of reconciliation. We are therefore Christ's ambassadors. It is as if God were appealing to you through us: we implore you in Christ's name, be reconciled to God!" (2 Cor. 5:19–20, REB).

But no absolute rules or regulations or code of laws to prescribe our good works? None. We're free of that. Christian faith does have vast ethical implications. But finally this faith is faith in Christ, not in an ethic. This is why it's called "Christ-ian." There is, however, one very common-sensible warning that follows as the night the day: that there's something definitely wrong if we try to serve the God of love unlovingly:

> For you were called to freedom, brothers and sisters; only do not use your freedom as an opportunity for self-indulgence, but through love become slaves to one another. For the whole law is summed up in a single commandment, "You shall love your neighbor as yourself."
>
> Galatians 5:13–14, NRSV

Bonhoeffer provides a wonderful gloss on what it means, from the Christian perspective, to "love your neighbor as yourself." He said, "Only unbelief can wish to give the world something less than Christ."[33]

This, then, is Christian freedom: to live for the single overruling purpose of making known the love of God made known by Christ. "Let all things be done for edification," said Paul (1 Cor. 14:26). Thus all Christians become "good news-ists." In one way or another, they are all evangel-ists, but never legalists.

19. A Literal Hell Means a Flaw in the Bible's Ointment

> *"Jesus said to them, 'You are mistaken, and surely this is the reason: you do not know either the scriptures or the power of God.' "*
>
> —Mark 12:24, NEB

False gods can never make us deeply happy. From the first day of our relationship with them, we live with the deep, gnawing fear and anxiety that they are false and may at any time forsake us. But, as we've said, it isn't until they actually do abandon us that we then must desperately look for something else to live for or worship or cling to—even if it's only something as briefly and unsatisfyingly helpful as Peppermint Patty's nose.

If and when this experience of the death of the old gods finally does occur, this is "hell," and it only occurs by the power of God—that is, by the power God has to destroy our false foundations and to turn our worship to him. This is why the Bible can refer to God as "the Destroyer" (e.g., 1 Cor. 10:6–10).

This is also why we now return to the saying of Jesus that relates the power of God to understanding scripture—that remarkable statement with which we began our meditations and which we now quote from another translation and from another Gospel. As Jesus indicates in this statement, not everyone knows the experience of the power of God. But without it we can very easily misunderstand the meaning of scripture. And whenever the New Testament talks about hell, it's absolutely necessary to know this experience in order to understand. This is because hell *is* the power of God. Hell is God's power as it acts upon us in this lifetime in this particular way. This is also why hell is "eternal"—that is, it's a direct confrontation with "the command of the eternal God, to bring about obedience of faith" (Rom. 16:26). Hell and the devil are the flip side, the dark and negative side, of the presence of God's Holy Spirit in our hearts. "Hell" is the way we *feel* without this Spirit; "the devil" is a first-century personification for the things we *do* without this Spirit. The two are closely related because desperate unhappiness (or "hell") tends to produce desperate evil (or the "d-evil"). For example, it's sometimes possible to see Lucy as a little Lucifer in whom the real biblical meaning of both hell and the devil, and their relationship, are delightfully dramatized.

But suppose we read about hell in the Bible and we don't

know this experience that belongs very much to this life—the experience of the power of God. Suppose we don't "know the tortures of the memory of a lost love"—an idolatrous love. Naturally we'll be inclined to understand hell as an experience that occurs way off in a future life somewhere.

Suppose we haven't had this horrifying experience in which God, completely against our own wills, forcefully wrenches us from the pitiful little false gods we're so strongly attached to. Then we'll naturally feel that anyone at any time, very much by their own "free wills," can know and follow God just as easily as a snap of the fingers.

On the other hand, suppose we *do* know this experience in which we have been forced, altogether against our own natural desires and wishes, to give up the old god and to serve the new one. Then we'll know we're not any better than anyone else. We'll know then we have only been one of the "objects of [God's] mercy" (Rom. 9:24, REB). We'll be able to look at the vilest, meanest person ever to walk the earth and say quite sincerely and thankfully, "There but by the grace of God go I!" We'll know we don't have anything that wasn't *completely* a gift to us. "What do you possess that was not given you? If then you really received it all as a gift, why take the credit to yourself?" (1 Cor. 4:7, NEB). We'll know there's no way in which we, more than anyone else, deserve to know this wonderful new God. And therefore we'll also be greatly inclined to be far more understanding and far less harsh and judgmental about other people and their problems.

See what happens? Knowing the power of God, we're able to appreciate, understand, and take with utmost seriousness everything the New Testament says about hell, but we're also able to appreciate, understand, and take with utmost gratitude everything the New Testament says about the gracious God "whose will it is that all should find salvation and come to know the truth" (1 Tim. 2:4, REB). The radical inconsistency between hell and God's grace vanishes. Otherwise, hell denies everything the New Testament tells us about God's grace—his infinite love and power. The conversation goes like this: "You say there is an eternal damnation when God our Father loves us so much and also is completely in charge? Get out of here! Oh, but we choose hell by our own free wills! Oh? There is free will when God is God and in complete control? And then *we choose* to damn ourselves to hell? What kind of sense does that make?" Depend on it: As soon as a literal hell is taken seriously, God's grace isn't. A literal hell means an inconsistent Bible. A literal hell means there is an inherent contradiction or serious flaw (or "fly"; Eccles. 10:1) in the Bible's ointment. And make no mistake: Whenever this fly/flaw appears, Christian faith gets seriously burned by it.

And so, then, this knowing or not knowing the power of God produces two radically different understandings of the Christian faith: one characterized by belief in God's *grace*, the love and the power by which God the Father, by his own gracious choice revealed in Christ, will finally save all of the children he has created; the other characterized by *law*, in which people, by their own wills, either save themselves or (for reasons not fully understood) damn themselves forever and ever.

But even if we may not know the power of God, and even if we do tend to take everything in scripture quite literally, the Bible is still plainly strong enough, in its overarching emphasis on the love of God, to create a context that can absorb any incompatible threat of God's everlasting hot temper. This being the case, why is it that the legalistic gloom-and-doom interpreters of the Bible have always seemed to have an upper hand in the church's history? If the Bible itself is so overwhelming in its emphasis on the grace of God, why does it often seem that the anger and judgment and vengeance of God are about all we're able to hear from so many different churches and preachers?

The answer to this question is really very simple; it's exactly the same answer we discovered for the question of why free will always seems to be such a popular idea when it's obviously denied by the Bible. We might have easily guessed this answer, knowing what we do from Christ's revelation about the nature of men and women. The basic reason behind the popularity of both of these nonbiblical ideas, free will and a literal hell, is *sin*. Both of them are immensely ego-enhancing. If I have free will, I am the master of my fate and captain of my soul. Finally, then, I'm my own god. So don't tell me I don't have free will! That's the ultimate put-down to my pride!

The same thing applies to a literal hell. For if there is such a punishment, surely God is not going to subject us to it unless we've chosen it ourselves. So again, I turn out to be in control in the final analysis. In this way I can do the right thing and be very proud of myself; I'm also justified in feeling superior and looking down my nose with righteous hostility at other people who haven't made the right choice. What could possibly be more ego-enhancing? It's the good and righteous people who have made "themselves righteous," versus all the miserable sinners who have no one to blame but themselves. Therefore I am much better than they. And so in comes free will and a literal hell, and out goes the grace of God. And isn't that wonderful? It makes me feel so good!

But what about those occasional folks who believe in a literal hell and yet aren't so fully convinced that they're good enough to avoid it? I like the way John Donne has answered this group:

"Even in this inordinate dejection thou exaltest thy self above God, and makest thy worst better than his best, thy sins larger than his mercy."[34] One way or another, belief in a literal hell always seems to mean, "I'm the best!"

And just as *individuals* can use free will and a literal hell to build themselves up, so can *institutions*. Soon after churches found out they could regulate people's moral behavior by vague threats of hellfire, they discovered they could control just about everything else in exactly the same way, especially by making the threats less vague. With the "keys" to the kingdom of God in their hands, the churches put themselves in charge of people's personal piety, their pocketbooks, and their politics. Hellfire was the fuel that ran most of the medieval church and most of the lives of the people connected to it. The gospel of God's love became "the gospel at gunpoint."[35] The good news became the bad news. "Spiritual terrorism" became the order of the day. Is it any wonder that this church became such a huge, strong, worldly power? Do what we say, or your soul will writhe in agony for all eternity! One must admit that this kind of threat will slow you down, regardless of where it comes from!

We mustn't think that threats like this aren't still widely used today. One summer Peppermint Patty and Marcie showed up at what was evidently a church-sponsored camp for kids. And there "speakers" bombarded them with much talk about the imminent end of the world. This was very disturbing to Peppermint Patty until she realized what was behind all of this frightening talk of doom and damnation.

The threats of a literal hell will probably always be with us for the very reason that sin and selfishness will always be with us. But this understanding of Christian faith must be resisted, not only because it's not true but also because of all of the *real* hell it causes right here and now in this life. Russian theologian Nicholas Berdyaev once wrote, "I can conceive of no more powerful and irrefutable argument in favor of atheism than the eternal torments of hell."[36]

And this means atheism in all its many forms. For instance, it was their revolt against this "traditional" teaching of the churches that made atheists out of Friedrich Nietzsche and Richard Wagner (Wagner, the great composer but lousy philosopher), who in turn went a long way in producing Hitler; and we know what *he* produced. It was their revulsion from this teaching that made atheists out of people like Feuerbach, Marx,

Engels, Lenin, and Stalin; and we know what *they* produced. But other leaders, who also don't come close to believing in God, can hypocritically *support* the teaching of a literal hell simply in order to make obedient and compliant sheep out of the people they rule. And then there's the widespread grass-roots atheism of ordinary men and women who have simply grown indifferent to any "heavenly Father" who is generally understood to be all-loving and all-powerful and yet is inconsistently going to send so many of his own children packing off to a meaningless hell.

Hell "meaningless"? Of course! For if people are in hell for all eternity, how can they ever put to use any lessons they may pick up there? What good would come from such suffering? The "Angelic Doctor," Thomas Aquinas, was asked what good purpose was served by all this agony. The best answer he could come up with was to say that eternal torment would furnish entertainment for the eternally blessed: "That the saints may enjoy their beatitude and the grace of God more abundantly, they are permitted to see the punishment of the damned in Hell."[37]

Some saints. Some God. But at least in this statement we should be able to see clearly why people often believe in such a God: to satisfy their own hateful and vindictive natures. Cruel gods and cruel people beget each other. On the other hand, any person who knows anything about the love of God revealed in Christ is going to be just as concerned about the final fate of the "losers" as of the "winners." If Christians should get to heaven and discover they are the only people there, they will have learned—by God's own love made known to them through Christ—to get up a petition drive to spring their brothers and sisters from hell.

"The victory that defeats the world is our faith" (1 John 5:4, NEB). There can be no "victory" worth the name when any of the children created and loved by God are finally defeated by a literal hell. In that case the world would have won.

But in the meantime a literal hell produces atheism or disbelief. And as Dostoevsky could say, "All evil [is] grounded upon disbelief."[38] People look at the false God of a literal hell and throw the baby out with the bathwater. And then this atheism produces nothing but the worship of other false gods of one kind or another. This is the major reason why there are so many phony gods around, and with such strong appeal nowadays. More than anything else, it's this weakness in Christian understanding that has produced the great number and strength of so many different idols. People have to have something to believe in.[39] And when the Christian God turns out to be such an ogre, why believe in it? Unless of course we're frightened into it and/or take great delight in our own righteousness.

Well, what can we learn from this sorry spectacle of Christianity's age-old tendency to bully people with the bugaboo of a literal hell? Many things, of course. But I believe one of the most important lessons comes from the saying of Jesus with which we began: In order to understand properly, two things are necessary—scrip-

ture and the power of God. It seems to me the churches haven't
really bothered all that much to address their message specifically
to those people who *know* the power of God, to those who are
actually going through hell in *this* lifetime. This is certainly the
group of people to whom the New Testament directs its message.
For these are the only people whose depth of experience actually
matches the depth of the Bible's message. People's *deepest* needs,
even among the very young, are always the best point of contact
for the Bible. For when people's questions don't correspond with
the depth of the Bible's answers, these answers will often be re-
jected, ignored, or translated into something as superficial as the
superficiality that listens to them. Then these answers can become distorted, weak, and ineffective, only possessing the power
to cause trouble. "Do not throw your pearls to the pigs," said
Jesus; "they will only trample on them, and turn and tear you to
pieces" (Matt. 7:6, NEB).

But when the message of scripture is directed to those who
really need it and for whom it was actually intended, the spiritually lowest of the low, then this message can be deeply and cor-
rectly heard, understood, and taken to heart. To go back to
Oscar Wilde's way of putting it, How else but through a broken
heart (a heart placed in hell by the power of God) can scripture
(and what it says about hell) be properly understood and appre-
ciated? When this finally begins to happen, then the good news
of the New Testament will indeed begin to sound "new and
improved":

> On that day the deaf will hear
> when a book is read,
> and the eyes of the blind will see
> out of impenetrable darkness.
> The lowly will once again rejoice in the LORD,
> and the poor exult in the Holy One of Israel.
>   Isaiah 29:18–19, REB

20. The Problem of Evil, or What's the Last Word?

"The grace of the Lord Jesus be with all."
—Revelation 22:21, REB

The problem of evil is simply this: Why does an all-loving and all-powerful God allow evil in his creation? Why is there sin and death and all kinds of suffering? Well, of course if we don't take this question too seriously we can always tell ourselves that evil is the fault of people. People always bring these things on themselves. But this of course is nonsense, because we can immediately see that people don't always cause death and other natural evils, like California's earthquakes and Chicago's weather. And anyway the Bible tells us that "sometimes the just person gets what is due to the unjust, and the unjust what is due to the just" (Eccles. 8:14, REB). As a matter of fact the Bible, rather than seeing people as the ultimate cause of evil, actually tells us that this is God's department:

> I am the LORD, and there is none else.
> I form the light, and create darkness:
> I make peace, and create evil:
> I the LORD do all these things.
> Isaiah 45:6–7, KJV

Well, then, that's the problem of evil. Why does God create this, too?

When we talk about faith's response to evil, it's possible to divide faith into two general types: childish and childlike. *Childish faith* is really a form of paganism. It says, "I'll believe in God as long as he meets my expectations and doesn't let me down. Otherwise he's out." In this scheme of things, God's purpose is to do *our* will, rather than our purpose being to do *God's* will. God had better be careful, or we'll dump him so fast it'll make his head spin. So a childish or pagan faith looks like this:

Childish faith, then, isn't really worship of God at all, as it turns out. It's worship of some material payoff that God is supposed to make. And when God doesn't pay off, he's dropped as the provider of what we really worship. God is just a means to this material end, the material end being our real god. A childish faith knows exactly how God is supposed to act. It will tell us for instance that "God tempers the wind to the shorn lamb." But this naïve thought is from a sentimental eighteenth-century

English novel,[40] not from the Bible. The Bible is a supremely realistic book. It knows that this is very often not the way things work out.

Childlike faith, on the other hand, actually trusts in God and not in those things we want God to give us. It is childlike precisely because of this element of simple trust that goes beyond material payoffs and appearances. And, rather than being turned *away* from God by evil, childlike faith is turned *to* God by evil. Childlike faith says, "I've got to trust in God. Everything else has either failed me or is in the process of failing me. God is the only hope I have." But this childlike hope, this "faith no bigger even than a mustard seed" (Matt. 17:20, NEB), finally is infinitely more satisfying to the human heart than all of the so-called "good things" we can accumulate in a life without hope in God.

And so real faith, rather than being threatened by evil, is strengthened by evil. Faith wouldn't even *be* faith without evil staring it in the face. Without evil, it would be knowledge. Faith knows what it knows in spite of appearances to the contrary. This is exactly what makes it faith and not knowledge. If we had a provable answer to the problem of evil, we wouldn't need faith. It is the very existence of evil that makes it necessary for us to live "by faith, not by sight" (2 Cor. 5:7). For "faith gives substance to our hopes, makes us certain of realities we do not see" (Heb. 11:1, NEB). And this is exactly the way God wants us to live. For faith is heart knowledge, not head knowledge. And God wants our relationship to him to be a relationship of the heart.

But faith, we must remember, is not just a kind of mental OK we grant to what we believe. It's active obedience on the basis of this belief, or else it's not really belief at all. What kind of "belief" or "faith" or "trust" in something would we have if we merely said OK to that something but didn't do anything about it? And so it is with faith in God. It's not really faith in God unless we obey God's command: to make known the love made known through Christ. And this means that faith's response to evil, if it really is faith, is to fight it, to resist it, to defy it, to seek to overcome it. Paul puts it this way: "Do not be overcome by evil, but overcome evil with good" (Rom. 12:21). Snoopy puts it this way:

This is how Christians resist or overcome evil. They react to the negative with the positive. They resist with the love they've found in Christ, which very often means—as far as this world goes—not to resist at all. Quoting the Old Testament, Jesus tells us:

> You have heard that it was said, "An eye for an eye and a tooth for a tooth." But I say to you, Do not resist one who is evil. But if any one

strikes you on the right cheek, turn to him the other also.

Matthew 5:38–39

In this way Christians witness to the only power finally strong enough to overcome evil: God's love.

But now, one more word about the *quality* of God's love revealed in Jesus. If this love is not finally victorious over all evil, then God finally is not a God of grace, all-loving and all-powerful. If the purpose and plan of God are not finally fulfilled, then obviously God has failed. Finally, God's will has not been done. And in this case, what kind of God is this? Certainly not the God of grace claimed by the entire New Testament. And when God is so disgraceful, we're left with an alternative: either the threat of a meaningless hell, in which people can choose to be tortured for all eternity to no good purpose; or else, rejecting a meaningless hell, a meaningless life without any God—a life that may follow "the paths of glory"[41] for a very little while but then finally ends only in the grave. If death and the grave have the last word, then life—by definition—is meaningless. It isn't going anywhere. And a meaningless life makes people mean. Ultimately having no future, we may as well get all we can while we can. Thus meaninglessness doth make vicious little vermin of us all. Rats, in other words.

In our sillier moments we may try to tell ourselves that the gift of life should be satisfying enough for anyone who has known it, and that it's selfish of us to want more. Save this beautiful thought. Save it for the four-year-old with leukemia you may run into. And in the meantime, take note of this from Paul:

> How can some of you say there is no resurrection of the dead? If there be no resurrection, then Christ was not raised; and if Christ was not raised, then our gospel is null and void, and so is your faith. . . . If it is for this life only that Christ has given us hope, we of all men are most to be pitied.
>
> 1 Corinthians 15:12–14, 19, NEB

But of course in this case *everyone* is to be pitied. For the more beautiful life may have been, the sadder it'll be to leave it. And this sadness is easy to feel long before the end. It really isn't very good news to tell someone, "It just doesn't get any better than this."

But Christians are a people who believe firmly in God's grace, and therefore they are persuaded that God's purpose and plan will finally be fulfilled. And that plan and purpose is good news—the best possible news—for all. Once more, the words of Paul:

> In Christ our release is secured and our sins are forgiven through the shedding of his blood. Therein lies the richness of God's free grace lavished upon us, imparting full wisdom and insight. He has made known to us his hidden purpose—such was his will and pleasure determined beforehand in Christ—to be put into effect when the time was ripe: namely, that the universe, all in heaven and on earth, might be brought into a unity in Christ.
>
> Ephesians 1:7–10, NEB

This is faith's final answer to evil, then, the answer that the universe, everything and everyone in heaven and earth, will finally be brought into a unity in Christ. This answer doesn't really clear up the question of "Why evil in the first place?" But if we knew the answer to that one "we would be in eternal life," as Bonhoeffer could say.[42] Nevertheless this answer does assure us that finally all evil—all sin, death, and suffering—will be overcome. And therefore faith can also say with Paul, "I consider that the sufferings of this present time are not worth comparing with the glory that is to be revealed to us" (Rom. 8:18).

The late William Barclay, the great Scottish Bible teacher and scholar, tells us in his autobiography, "I believe that in the end all men will be gathered into the love of God." And he goes on to point out that in supporting this case, "The New Testament itself is not in the least afraid of the word *all*."[43] Especially in Paul's writings there are plenty of places where he can't seem to cram enough "all's" into what he wants to say. For example, he looks forward to the time when

God has put all enemies under [Christ's] feet; and the last enemy to be deposed is death . . . and when all things are subject to him, then the Son himself will also be made subject to God who made all things subject to him, and thus God will be all in all.

1 Corinthians 15:25–26, 28, REB

So all in all, the Bible tells us we know through faith in Christ that God will finally be all in all. The Bible's last word is "all." Sin, evil, suffering, death, and a literal hell are finally conquered by this literal "all": "The grace of the Lord Jesus be with all" (Rev. 22:21, REB). That's the Bible's punch line. Or, as another translation has it, "May the grace of the Lord Jesus be with everyone" (TEV). God has promised to answer this prayer of his people. And surely we can expect at least as much from God as God expects from us. Again, the words of Jesus:

But what I tell you is this: Love your enemies and pray for your persecutors; only so can you be children of your heavenly Father, who causes the sun to rise on good and bad alike, and sends the rain on the innocent and the wicked. . . . There must be no limit to your goodness, as your heavenly Father's goodness knows no bounds.

Matthew 5:44–45, 48, REB

Notes

1. James D. Smart, *The Strange Silence of the Bible in the Church: A Study in Hermeneutics* (Philadelphia: Westminster Press, 1970), p. 10.
2. Ibid., p. 144.
3. E. D. Hirsch, Jr., *Cultural Literacy: What Every American Needs to Know* (Boston: Houghton Mifflin Co., 1987).
4. George Steiner, "The Good Books," in *The New Yorker*, Jan. 11, 1988, p. 94.
5. Charles Schulz, "Meet the Creator of Peanuts," *Christian Business Men's Committee Contact*, vol. 25, no. 2 (Feb. 1967), p. 6.
6. David Freedberg, *The Power of Images* (Chicago: University of Chicago Press, 1989), ch. 8.
7. Quoted in Ewald M. Plass, comp., *What Luther Says*, vol. III (Saint Louis: Concordia Publishing House, 1959), p. 1129.
8. See Roland H. Bainton, *Here I Stand: A Life of Martin Luther* (New York: Mentor Books, 1950), p. 238.
9. From "Luther's Preface to *Aesop's Fables*," quoted in *Early Protestant Educators*, ed. Frederick Eby (New York: McGraw-Hill Book Co., 1931), pp. 153–154.
10. N. H. Kleinbaum, *Dead Poets Society* (New York: Bantam Books, 1989), pp. 38–39. This novel is based on the motion picture with screenplay written by Tom Schulman.
11. Oscar Wilde, "The Ballad of Reading Gaol," quoted in *The Literature of England*, ed. G. B. Woods et al. (Chicago: Scott, Foresman & Co., 1948), p. 891.
12. *The Confessions of St. Augustine*, book I, ch. 1.
13. Søren Kierkegaard, *Concluding Unscientific Postscript* (Princeton: Princeton University Press, 1944), p. 169.
14. Steiner, "The Good Books," p. 97.
15. Karl Barth, *Church Dogmatics*, vol. II/2, Authorised Translation (Edinburgh: T. & T. Clark, 1957), p. 88.
16. Quoted in Ralph Waldo Emerson, "The Comic," in *Theories of Comedy*, ed. Paul Lauter (Garden City: Doubleday & Co., Anchor Books, 1964), p. 378.
17. "For the Time Being: A Christmas Oratorio," *The Collected Poetry of W. H. Auden*, ed. Edward Mendelson (New York: Random House, 1976), p. 412.
18. See my book on Ecclesiastes, *A Time to Be Born—A Time to Die* (New York: Harper & Row, 1973), especially Parts II and III.
19. As an undergraduate, I once drove a fraternity brother to the local train station, where he began the trip on which he was killed. My intelligent and sensitive friend was an atheist, as I also had been, and this had led to many lively discussions between us. But I'll never forget his final words to me over our parting handshake: "If there is a God, why didn't he make it so we could shake *his* hand?" In this statement I believe my friend expressed a universal human desire or need: our need to meet God *in history*. Christian faith believes that in Christ, God accommodated himself to this need.
20. Karl Barth, *The Faith of the Church*, ed. Jean-Louis Leaba, tr. Gabriel Vahanian (New York: Meridian Books, 1958), p. 63.

21. Fyodor Dostoevsky, *The Brothers Karamazov,* tr. Constance Garnett (New York: Modern Library, 1950), book VI, ch. III, i.
22. Dietrich Bonhoeffer, *Ethics,* ed. Eberhard Bethge, tr. Neville Horton Smith (New York: Macmillan Publishing Co., 1955), p. 204.
23. Quoted in Dietrich Bonhoeffer, *The Cost of Discipleship,* rev. ed., tr. R. H. Fuller (New York: Macmillan Publishing Co., 1963), p. 277.
24. Franz Kafka, "A Report to an Academy," *Selected Short Stories,* tr. Willa and Edwin Muir (New York: Modern Library, 1952), p. 173.
25. The phrase is suggested by Dostoevsky's "The Grand Inquisitor," from *The Brothers Karamazov,* widely believed to be the greatest novel ever written and certainly an incomparable explication of genuine Christian faith.
26. The best discussion I know of this subject is the entire volume of Barth's *Church Dogmatics,* IV/4, "Baptism as the Foundation of the Christian Life."
27. Quoted in John Dillenberger and Claude Welch, *Protestant Christianity Interpreted Through Its Development* (New York: Charles Scribner's Sons, 1954), p. 56.
28. See William J. Wolf's excellent book on Lincoln, *Lincoln's Religion* (Philadelphia: Pilgrim Press, 1970), in particular pp. 95 and 152.
29. For instance, American historian Herbert J. Muller can point to the spread of democracy in the nineteenth century: "[Protestantism's] basic principles of individualism and of 'protest' against any human authority claiming absolute right were naturally more conducive to the growth of a free society; it kept breeding dissenters, nonconformists, rebels. It was in fact the dominant religion in all the major countries except France that made the most marked advance toward democracy . . . . " (*Religion and Freedom in the Modern World* [Chicago: The University of Chicago Press, 1963], p. 15).
30. Sally Brown is alluding in this cartoon to Ecclesiastes 12:2–6, the "Allegory of Old Age." For Ecclesiastes also had little hope for anything beyond the grave. So Sally could have just as well yelled, "A living dog is better than a dead lion!"
31. Kafka, "A Report to an Academy."
32. Snoopy's quote is from Alexander Pope's poem "Eloisa to Abelard."
33. Bonhoeffer, *Ethics,* p. 206.
34. *The Complete Poetry and Selected Prose of John Donne,* ed. Charles M. Coffin (New York: Modern Library, 1952), p. 481.
35. The phrase is Karl Barth's description of a sermon by Billy Graham (Eberhard Busch, *Karl Barth: His Life From Letters and Autobiographical Texts,* tr. John Bowden [Philadelphia: Fortress Press, 1976], p. 446).
36. Nicholas Berdyaev, *Dream and Reality: An Essay in Autobiography,* tr. Katherine Lampert (New York: Macmillan Publishing Co., 1950), p. 293.
37. Quoted in *The World Treasury of Religious Quotations,* ed. Ralph L. Woods (New York: Hawthorn Books, 1966), p. 429.
38. Fyodor Dostoevsky, *Letters of Fyodor Dostoevsky to His Family and Friends,* tr. Ethel Colburn Mayne (New York: McGraw-Hill, 1964), p. 257.
39. See my book *Something to Believe In* (New York: Harper & Row, 1978).
40. Laurence Sterne, *A Sentimental Journey Through France and Italy,* ed. Graham Petrie (New York: Penguin Books, 1967).
41. Marcie's quote is from Thomas Gray's poem "Elegy in a Country Churchyard."
42. Dietrich Bonhoeffer, *No Rusty Swords,* ed. Edwin H. Robertson and John Bowden (New York: Harper & Row, 1965), p. 143.
43. William Barclay, *A Spiritual Autobiography* (Grand Rapids: Wm. B. Eerdmans Publishing Co., 1975), pp. 58–59.

Acknowledgments

Unless otherwise identified, scripture quotations are from the Revised Standard Version of the Bible, copyrighted 1946, 1952, © 1971, 1973 by the Division of Christian Education of the National Council of the Churches of Christ in the U.S.A., and are used by permission.

Scripture quotations marked NRSV are from the New Revised Standard Version of the Bible and are copyrighted © 1989 by the Division of Christian Education of the National Council of Churches of Christ in the U.S.A., and are used by permission.

Scripture quotations marked NEB are taken from *The New English Bible,* © The Delegates of the Oxford University Press and The Syndics of the Cambridge University Press, 1961, 1970. Used by permission.

Scripture quotations marked REB are taken from *The Revised English Bible,* © Oxford University Press and Cambridge University Press, 1989. Used by permission.

Scripture quotations marked JB are from The Jerusalem Bible, copyright © 1966, 1967, 1968 by Darton, Longman, & Todd, Ltd., and Doubleday & Co., Inc. Used by permission of the publishers.

Scripture quotations marked NJB are from *The New Jerusalem Bible,* copyright © 1985 by Darton, Longman & Todd, Ltd., and Doubleday, a division of Bantam Doubleday Dell Publishing Group, Inc. Reprinted by permission of the publishers.

Scripture quotations marked TEV are from the *Good News Bible*—Old Testament: Copyright © American Bible Society 1976; New Testament: Copyright © American Bible Society 1966, 1971, 1976.

The quotation in Meditation 13 from "For the Time Being: A Christmas Oratorio," by W. H. Auden, in *W. H. Auden: Collected Poems,* ed. Edward Mendelson (New York: Random House, 1976), copyright 1976 by Edward Mendelson and Monroe K. Spears, is used by permission of the publisher.

CPSIA information can be obtained
at www.ICGtesting.com
Printed in the USA
LVOW13s0342120818
586687LV00011B/514/P

9 780664 251529